Nigel Pearce

Photo credits

p1 (top) © Farknot Architect/Shutterstock, (bottom) © Yuri Arcurs/Adobe Stock; **p5** (left) © Anne Kitzman/Shutterstock, (middle) © Elwynn/Shutterstock, (left) © Cristovao/Shutterstock; **p7** © RnDmS/Shutterstock; **p9** © Lena Serditova/Shutterstock; **p14** © connel/ Shutterstock; **p17** © Dmytro Shapoval/Shutterstock; **p19** © Delphotostock/Adobe Stock; **p21** © Juriaan Wossink/Shutterstock; **p23** (left) © Soloviova Liudmyla/Shutterstock, (middle) © AHPhotosWPG/Shutterstock, (right) © NinaMalyna/Adobe Stock; **p29** (left) © Yanlev/Adobe Stock, (right) © Kalim/Adobe Stock; **p30** © WitR/Adobe Stock; **p31** © spotmatikphoto/Adobe Stock; **p36** © Ingram Publishing Limited/Scenery Platinum Vol 2 CD 5; **p38** © ti_to_tito/Adobe Stock; **p39** © Ozgur Coskun/Adobe Stock; **p40** © therabbithole/Adobe Stock; **p45** © ercan senkaya/Adobe Stock; **p46** © BillionPhotos.com/Adobe Stock; **p51** © Alexander Raths/ Adobe Stock; **p52** © Africa Studio/Adobe Stock; **p56** © Arpad Nagy-Bagoly/Adobe Stock; **p58** (row 1 from left to right) © Stockbyte/ Photolibrary Group Ltd/ Sports Elements E0002, © Maksim Toome/Shutterstock, © fizkes/Adobe Stock, (row 2 from left to right) © Monika Chodak/Shutterstock, © Esin Deniz/Adobe Stock, © Imagestate Media (John Foxx) / Amazing Animals Vol 26, (row 3 from left to right) © Philip Lange/Shutterstock, © bertys30/Adobe Stock, © Philip Lange/Shutterstock, (row 5 from left to right) ©Tony Gable and C Squared Studios/Photodisc/Getty Images/Musical Instruments 34, © GaudiLab/Shutterstock, © Africa Studio/Adobe Stock; **p60** © janoka82/Adobe Stock; **p61** (left) © Phillip Minnis/Shutterstock (right) © Olga Nayashkova/Adobe Stock; **p69** © Aaltair/ Shutterstock; **p78** © Dusan Kostic/Adobe Stock; **p79** (top left) © Steve Mason/Photodisc/Getty Images/ Eat, Drink, Dine 48, (top middle) © Tyler Olson/Adobe Stock, (top right) © goodluz/Adobe Stock (top left), (bottom left) © Gorillaimages/Shutterstock, (bottom right) © Kent Knudson/Photodisc/Getty Images/ Environmental Concerns 31; **p81** © goldenangel/Adobe Stock; **p83** © Rrrainbow/ Shutterstock; **p88** © Amfroey/Shutterstock; **p91** © dacosta/123RF; **p93** © travelview/Adobe Stock; **p101** (top left) © Elenathewise/ Adobe Stock, (top middle) © akeeris/Adobe Stock, (top right) © Stockbyte/Getty Images / Design Essentials E0005, (bottom left) © sonya etchison/Adobe Stock, (bottom middle) © Imagestate Media (John Foxx) / Vol 08 Modern Lifestyles, (bottom right) © Ingram Publishing Limited / Sport Mark Maziarz Master Series; **p103** © Leonid Andronov/Shutterstock; p107 © SkyLine/Adobe Stock; **p109** © Diego Cervo/Adobe Stock; **p110** © oneinchpunch/Adobe Stock

Orders: **Teachers** please contact Bookpoint Ltd, 130 Park Drive, Milton Park, Abingdon, Oxon OX14 4SE. Telephone: (44) 01235 400555. Email primary@bookpoint.co.uk. Lines are open from 9 a.m. to 5 p.m., Monday to Saturday, with a 24-hour message answering service.

Parents, Tutors please call: 020 3122 6405 (Monday to Friday, 9:30 a.m. to 4.30 p.m.).

Email: parentenquiries@galorepark.co.uk

Visit our website at www.galorepark.co.uk for details of other revision guides for Common Entrance, examination papers and Galore Park publications.

ISBN: 978 1 4718 6724 8

First published in 2018 by
Galore Park Publishing Ltd,
An Hachette UK Company
Carmelite House
50 Victoria Embankment
London EC4Y 0DZ

www.galorepark.co.uk

Impression number 10 9 8 7 6 5 4 3 2 1

Year 2022 2021 2020 2019 2018

Cover photo © Nataliya Hora/123RF.co

Typeset in ITC Officina Sans Std book 11.5/13 by Integra Software Services Pvt. Ltd., Pondicherry, India

Printed in Dubai by Oriental Press Ltd

A catalogue record for this title is available from the British Library.

Table des matières

Notes on features in this book

Exam style Exercice

Exam-style exercises have been included to help you familiarise yourself with the format of the exam. Where these are specific to either Level 1 or 2, the following icons are used. All other exam-style exercises are relevant for both levels.

Level 1 exercises **Level 1**

Level 2 exercises **Level 2**

Exercises originally designed for specific skills are shown by these symbols, although, of course, many exercises can be used in several different ways.

Listening 

Speaking 

Reading 

Writing 

Introduction

About this book

French for Common Entrance Two completes the *French for Common Entrance* course. It is designed to provide enough practice in Common Entrance French to challenge high achievers, as well as providing all students with a thorough grounding in the basics. *French for Common Entrance* will therefore also serve as a good basis for those wanting to move on to more advanced study and take French in the Common Academic Scholarship exams, although teachers will be well aware that schools setting their own papers will have different requirements, reflected in their examinations' format.

1 C'est comment?

This chapter, and the next, will help you understand people's opinions about the places they go and the things they do; you will also begin to learn about **comparison**.

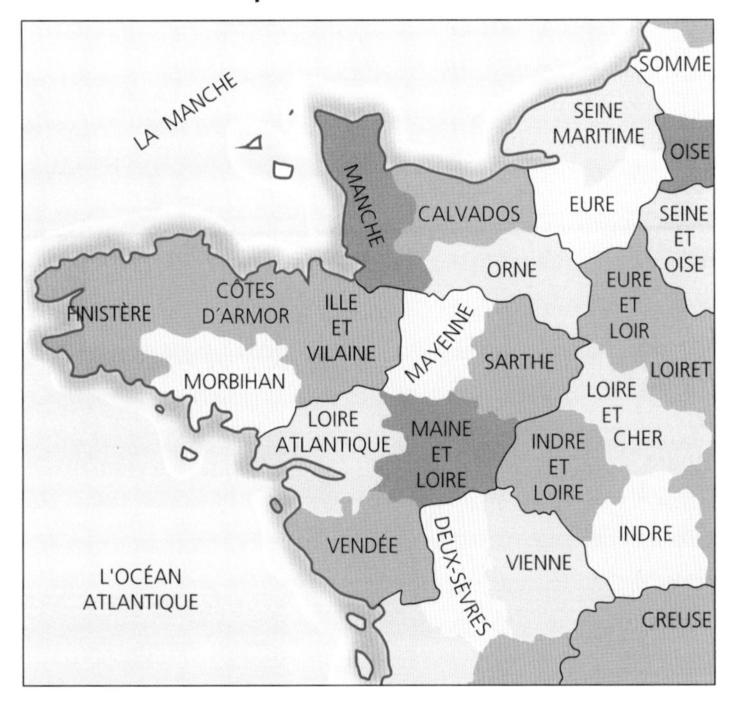

Les départements et les régions

Just as in the UK we have counties (for example Kent and Lancashire) and areas (for example the Highlands and East Anglia), France is divided up into départements and régions. There are 101 départements. At one time there were many more régions (up to 27) but, for administrative reasons, these were reduced in 2016 to 13 (for mainland France and Corsica), when several were combined into larger ones. Most départements and régions are in mainland France (France métropolitaine), but some are overseas.

Vendée is a département, situated in the Pays de la Loire région. For purposes such as postcodes, each département has a number, based on alphabetical order. Var is 84, Vendée is 85 and Vienne is 86, for example.

A postcode will feature this number, followed by three more figures. La Roche-sur-Yon is the 'capital' of Vendée and has the postcode 85000.

Exercice 1.1

La boîte en argent (suite)

Study the vocabulary, then listen to the audio and do the exercise that follows.

je ne sais plus	I don't know any more
ne ... plus	no more, no longer
la documentation	the paperwork
un tiroir	a drawer
un bureau	a study, a desk
quand même	after all, anyway
une serviette	a briefcase
lui	to him, to her
pauvre	poor
le sud	the south
l'année dernière	last year
se souvenir (de) (*irregular, like* venir)	to remember
les gosses	the kids
les nouvelles	the news
la Belgique	Belgium
elle a l'air triste	she looks sad

Choose the correct word to complete each sentence.

1 Peter is ...'s email correspondent. (Magali/Chloé)

2 Peter is coming to France in ... (October/September/August)

3 Albertine is an old friend of ... (Magali/Maman/Mamie)

4 Albertine probably now lives in ... (Belmont/Belgrade/Belgium)

5 When speaking, Mamie seems ... (lively/distant/sad)

C'est comment? – What is it like?

Understanding basic descriptions of events and places

In text, you may come across people describing places they have been to or experiences they have had. You will often hear c'est ... ('it's ...'):

Je vais à Paris; **c'est** formidable!	I'm going to Paris – it's brilliant!
Je vais au Futuroscope: **c'est** passionnant!	I'm going to Futuroscope: it's exciting!

Here are some 'opinion' words that can follow c'est:

passionnant	exciting
intéressant	interesting
formidable	brilliant
agréable	pleasant
bizarre	strange
amusant	fun
ennuyeux	boring
affreux	ghastly
sympa	nice
moche	ugly

Exercice 1.2

Translate these opinions into English:

1 Visiter Angers, c'est formidable!

2 Un repas au restaurant, c'est délicieux!

3 Faire les magasins avec Chloé, c'est amusant!

4 Faire du ski dans les Alpes, c'est passionnant!

5 Visiter le musée du Louvre, c'est intéressant!

Exercice 1.3

Listen as you read.

Chloé et Magali sont de nouveau* chez Mamie.

Chloé.	Bonjour, Mamie. Qu'est-ce que c'est?
Mamie.	Bonjour, les enfants. Ça? C'est une lettre.
Magali.	Alors?
Mamie.	Ce n'est pas Albertine qui m'écrit.
Chloé.	Ah bon, pourquoi? Elle est morte?

Mamie.	Mais non! Mais elle n'habite plus en Belgique.
Magali.	Chouette! Elle est en France!
Mamie.	Non plus. Elle habite à l'étranger.
Chloé.	À l'étranger! Zut!
Mamie.	C'est un voisin qui m'écrit.
Magali.	Qu'est-ce qu'il dit, le voisin? Où est-elle?
Mamie.	Le voisin n'a pas son adresse. Mais on ne sait jamais ...
* de nouveau	again

In the dialogue above, find the French expressions for:

1 It is not Albertine who is writing to me.
2 Is she dead?
3 She no longer lives in Belgium.
4 What does he say?
5 You never know.

Exercice 1.4

Using Exercice 1.3 to help you, try writing in French:

1 It is not Chloé who is writing the message.
2 Is she French?
3 We no longer live in England.
4 What do they (*m.*) think?
5 One never finds the answers.

Direct object and subject pronouns

Level 1

Here is a reminder of the simple pronouns we have used so far:

Subject pronouns		**Object pronouns**	
je	I	me	me
tu	you (as a subject)	te	you (as an object)
il	he	le	him, it (*m.*)
elle	she	la	her, it (*f.*)
nous	we	nous	us
vous	you (*pl.*)	vous	you (*pl.*)
ils	they (*m.*)	les	them (*f.* or *m.*)
elles	they (*f.*)		

Exercice 1.5

Study the following examples and try repeating them several times to get used to the sound; then translate them into English:

1 Tu me regardes.
2 Il nous cherche.
3 Elle vous écoute.
4 Je te retrouve.*
5 Il les oublie.**

* retrouver	to meet (up with)
** oublier	to forget

For variety, change the pronouns in each sentence and see if they make sense! But remember, the order is always the same:

1 **subject** pronoun (je, tu, il, elle, etc.)
2 **object** pronoun (me, te, le, la, etc.)
3 verb

So far, you have learnt quite a few pronouns, all of which have a definite job to do; so they are all together in a clear table in the section on pronouns in the 'Grammar summary'. We must not forget the reflexive pronouns, so they are there as well.

La comparaison – How to compare people and things

Look at the pictures.

Tochiko est **plus** grande* **que** Mina, mais elle est **moins** grande **que** Pascal. Pascal est **plus** grand **que** Tochiko et Mina.

* Note that adjectives used for comparing agree with the word they refer to as usual.

Comparison (comparing things or people) is a good thing to be able to do when describing. In English we can often do this just by altering an adjective (for example 'it is colder than yesterday'). In French this does not happen. Instead there are three words to use, which can be put before nearly any adjective or adverb. They must be followed by que (or qu' before a vowel or silent 'h'):

plus (...) que/qu'	more (...) than
moins (...) que/qu'	less (...) than
aussi (...) que/qu'	as (...) as

Exercice 1.6

Translate the following sentences into French. Don't forget to make the adjectives agree, where necessary.

1 The restaurant is bigger than the café.	restaurant (*m.*), grand, café (*m.*)
2 Marie is taller than Pierre.	grand
3 Your brother is smaller than my sister.	frère (*m.*), petit, sœur (*f.*)
4 In Paris it is* warmer than in** London.	Londres
5 February is colder than July.	février, froid, juillet

* weather: il fait … chaud

** in (+ city/town) = à

Exercice 1.7

Study the vocabulary before listening to the audio, then answer the questions.

comme avant	as before
une autoroute	a motorway
la mairie	the town hall, the mayor's office in a village
un parking	a car park
une église	a church
rouler	to go (in/on a wheeled vehicle)
monter à cheval	to ride on horseback
un feu	a fire
des feux	traffic lights
une école maternelle	a nursery school
une supérette	a mini-supermarket
une ferme	a farm
à cette époque-là	at that time
agricole	farming (*adj.*), agricultural

1 What is the first difference Mamie mentions?

2 In what way were people different?

3 Give two things that were *not* there when Mamie was young.

4 How many car parks are there in the village now?

5 Who had the only car when Mamie was young?

Exercice 1.8

Work in pairs. Help each other make a French sentence comparing two people (real or imaginary!). Use some of the adjectives below, or any others.

Be ready to say your sentence in class.

Remember the ways to compare people and things in French:

plus ... (adjective) ... que = more ... than;

moins ... (adjective) ... que = less ... than;

aussi ... (adjective) ... que = as ... as

For example:

Pauline est *aussi* grande *que* Claire.

Pauline is *as* tall *as* Claire.

intéressant/intéressante	moderne
actif/active	tolérant/tolérante
loyal/loyale	strict/stricte

Exercice 1.9

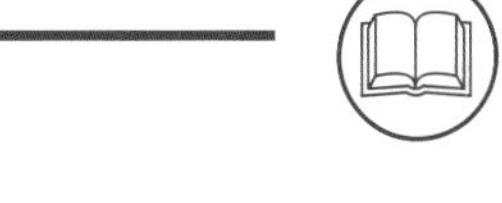

Read the passage aloud and then answer the questions.

Ce jour-là, Mamie continue à raconter les fêtes de sa jeunesse. Les enfants écoutent attentivement. Pendant qu'elle parle, Chloé et Magali essaient d'imaginer le village dans le passé. Magali veut poser des questions à Mamie sur la guerre. Mamie ne veut pas parler de cette période. Elle dit seulement que c'est une époque triste. Mais Chloé veut en savoir plus. Une fois rentrées à la maison, elles parlent de Mamie et de la boîte en argent, des fêtes au village, d'Albertine Lévy et du passé. Après le dîner, Chloé et Georges décident de faire

des recherches sur le village. Les filles essaient d'abord de trouver des informations sur internet, mais Chloé propose à sa sœur d'aller à Nantes chercher des informations à la bibliothèque.

aller chercher	to go and get
la jeunesse	youth
attentivement	attentively, carefully
pendant que	while
poser une question	to ask a question
la guerre	the war
curieux	curious
le passé	the past
faire des recherches	to do some research
proposer	to suggest
la bibliothèque	the library
une fois rentrées	once they had come home

Match the two halves of each sentence:

1 Mamie continue de parler
2 Pendant qu'elle parle,
3 Mamie dit que la guerre
4 Chloé veut en savoir plus
5 Elles ne trouvent pas assez

(a) sur la guerre et l'Occupation.
(b) des fêtes de sa jeunesse.
(c) d'informations sur internet.
(d) est une époque triste.
(e) elle a l'air triste.

Le centre-ville, c'est loin?

In this chapter, you will learn more to help you speak and write about finding your way in a French town or city and using transport.

Exercice 2.1

Listen as you read:

Chloé.	Zut! Il y a tellement de monde!
Magali.	Oui! Où est la bibliothèque?
Chloé.	Je ne sais pas. Je ne connais pas bien la ville.
Magali.	C'est vrai?
Chloé.	Je téléphone à Tochiko et je lui demande de venir.
Magali.	Pourquoi?
Chloé.	Pour nous aider.
Magali.	Super.

* * *

Magali.	Où est-ce qu'on la retrouve?
Chloé.	On a rendez-vous à dix heures, à l'office de tourisme.
Magali.	Chouette. Mais … où est l'office de tourisme?
Chloé.	Attends. Quelle heure est-il?

Magali.	C'est toi qui as la montre.
Chloé.	Tu m'embêtes. Ouf! La voilà. Il est dix heures moins dix.
Magali.	Donc, on a dix minutes.
Chloé.	J'ai une sœur intelligente.

tellement de monde	so many people
je lui demande de (+ *infin.*)	I ask her to ...
avoir rendez-vous	to have an arrangement to meet
embêter	to annoy

Now work in pairs. Prepare and perform the sketch.

Exercice 2.2

Choose a single word from the box below to fill each gap. One of the words given is not needed.

1 Magali et Chloé veulent ... la bibliothèque.

2 Chloé ... téléphoner à Tochiko.

3 À la gare, il y a ... de ...

4 Elles ... aller ... l'office de tourisme.

5 Tochiko ... être à l'office de ... à 10 h.

6 Chloé ... qu'elle ... une sœur intelligente.

tourisme	tellement	va
trouver	dit	à
vont	téléphone	monde
veut	a	

Exercice 2.3

Listen to the audio and check the vocabulary, then answer the questions in English.

pour aller à ...?	how do I get to...?
le/la plus proche	the nearest
ensuite	next (in a series of events)
en face de	opposite
de rien	you're welcome
désolé(e)	sorry
d'ici	from here
tu peux demander	you can ask
il y *en* a deux	there are two *of them*
loin	far, a long way

assez	quite; fairly
descendre de	to get off (a bus, etc.), to get out of (a car)
on y va?	shall we go?

1 Why can't the lady help them find their way?

2 How many tourist offices are there?

3 What is opposite the nearest tourist office?

4 How has Tochiko saved them time?

5 Where must they get off the tram?

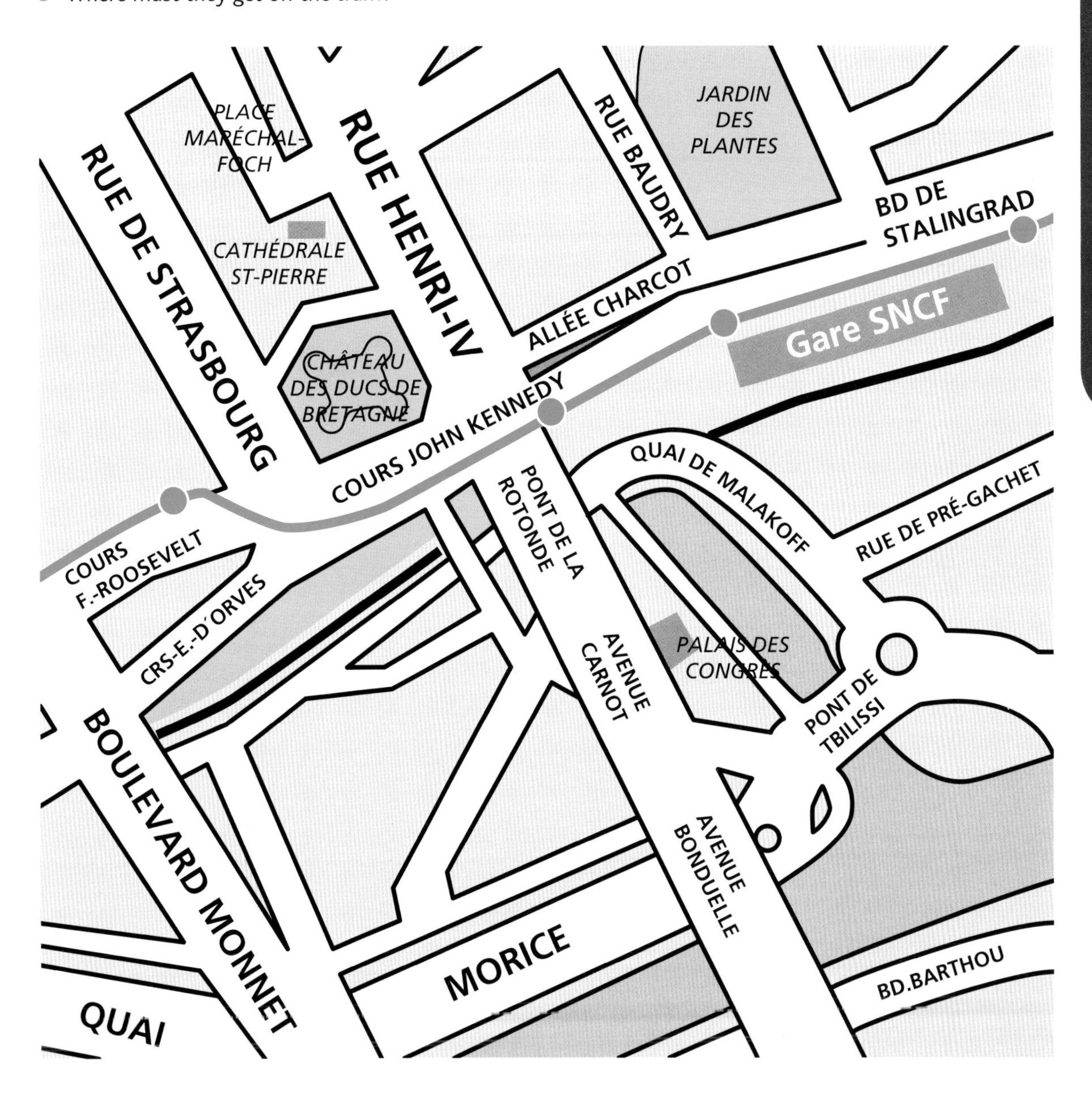

Les nombres ordinaux – Ordinal numbers

How to say first, second, third, and so on

When given, or giving, directions, we often need to say or understand 'the second on the right' or 'the first on the left', and so on. Here are some examples in English and French and how they are abbreviated when written or printed:

1st	premier, première	1er (*m.*), 1ère(*f.*)
2nd	deuxième	2e *or* 2ème
3rd	troisième	3e *or* 3ème
4th	quatrième	4e *or* 4ième

Exercice 2.4

Let's find our way!

Before you start, here are a few reminders:

à gauche	to/on the left
à droite	to/on the right
sur ta gauche/droite	on your left/right
tout droit	straight on
en face de	opposite
avant	before
devant	in front of
sur 100 mètres	for 100 metres
tourne, tournez	turn
va, allez	go
continue, continuez	go on, keep going
traverse, traversez	cross
prends, prenez	take
le long de	along

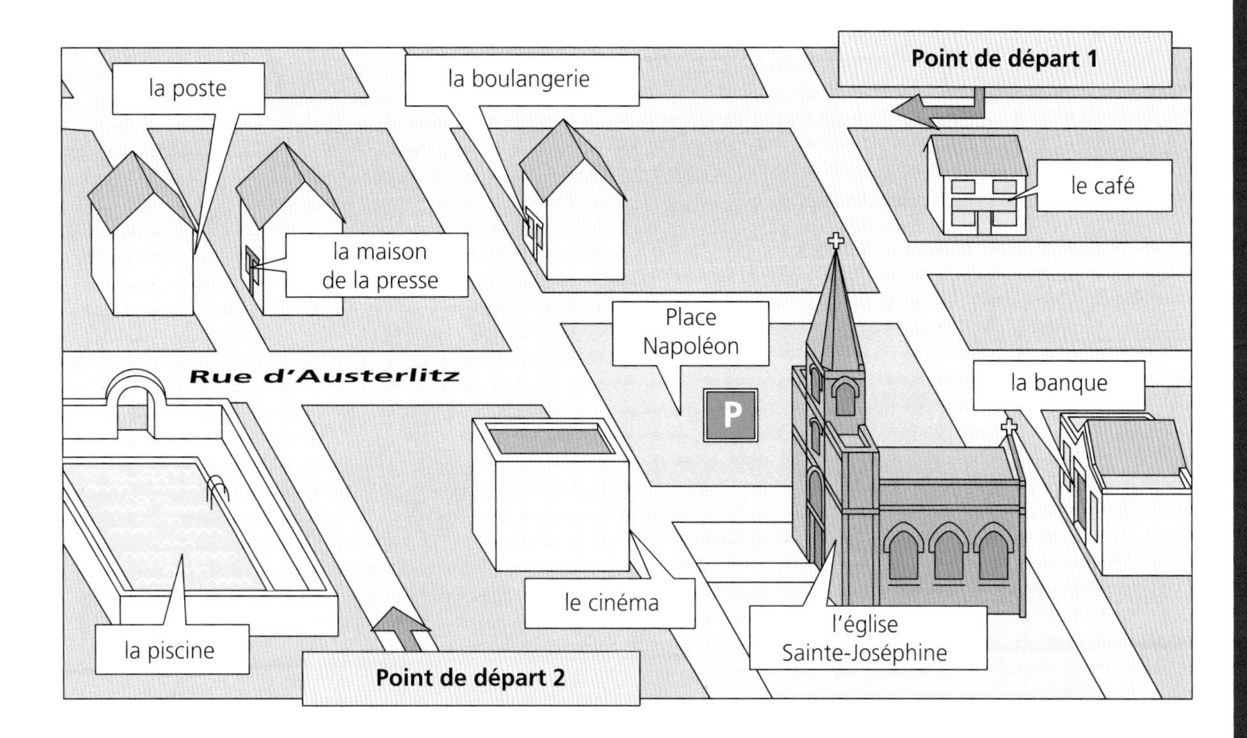

Look at the street map. Follow the directions from **starting point 1**. Where do they lead?

1 Va tout droit. Prends la deuxième rue à gauche. C'est sur ta gauche.

2 Prends la première rue à gauche. Traverse la Place Napoléon, c'est juste après le cinéma, à gauche.

3 Prends la rue à gauche, traverse le parking de la Place Napoléon, continue le long de la Rue d'Austerlitz, puis prends la première rue à droite. C'est en face de la poste.

4 Prends la rue à gauche. Continue sur 150 mètres. C'est en face de l'église.

Exercice 2.5

Try giving your own directions, from **starting point 2** on the map in Exercice 2.4, to these places:

1 à la boulangerie

2 à la poste

3 à l'église

4 à la banque

5 à la maison de la presse

Exercice 2.6

These sentences are all about people telling or asking other people to do things. Translate them into English.

1 Je demande à maman de m'aider.

2 Tu dis à papa de fermer la porte.

3 Elle dit à son frère de se lever.

4 Vous demandez au prof d'expliquer le dépliant*.

5 Chloé dit à Magali de parler à l'employé.

* un dépliant a leaflet

Pour aller plus loin ...

Translate into French:

6 She tells Paul to read the book.

7 We ask Jean to eat with us.

Exercice 2.7

Read this passage to yourself and out loud. Use the vocabulary below to ensure you understand it.

À la bibliothèque

Chloé, Magali et Tochiko sortent de l'office de tourisme et prennent le tramway pour aller à la bibliothèque. Après dix minutes, elles arrivent à l'université, où elles descendent. Elles demandent à un étudiant le chemin de la bibliothèque.

À l'intérieur, elles trouvent vite un gros livre avec l'histoire de leur village. Il est très intéressant et les filles passent deux heures à étudier l'histoire du village pendant les années 40, quand le village est occupé par les Allemands.

Au début, tout est assez calme. Il y a seulement un jeune soldat allemand dans le village. Mais plus tard, la situation devient difficile. Les occupants envoient beaucoup de jeunes hommes en Allemagne pour travailler. Ce système s'appelle Service de travail obligatoire (STO).

Chloé trouve une liste des personnes déportées. Sur la liste, elle lit le nom: Lévy, Jean-Paul. Toutes les trois quittent la bibliothèque. Elles achètent des tickets de bus et elles retournent au centre-ville où elles décident de déjeuner au McDo.

étudiant(e)	student
chemin (*m.*)	way
étudier	to study
soldat (*m.*)	soldier
allemand(e) (*adj.*)	German
Allemand(e) (*noun*)	German

Exercice 2.8

1 In the reading passage above, find the French expressions for:

(a) and (they) take the tram

(b) they get off

(c) they ask a student

(d) inside

(e) they quickly find

2 Vrai ou faux?

(a) The girls ask an old man the way to the university.

(b) There is a book in the library telling the history of the girls' village.

(c) Early in the war, many German soldiers lived in the village.

(d) Chloé finds a list of those taken away to work.

(e) The girls go home for lunch.

N'oublions pas les verbes! – Let's not forget the verbs!

You have now become used to using verbs in all sorts of different situations. Let's do some practice using the verbs that Chloé, Magali and Tochiko needed when they went to town. Make sure you know (that is, you can recite confidently!) their *present tense*.

aller	to go	chercher	to look for
trouver	to find	demander	to ask (for)
faire	to do, to make	lire	to read
tourner	to turn	traverser	to cross
continuer	to continue	prendre	to take

Exercice 2.9

Choose the correct form of the verb to complete each sentence, for example:

Elles … les magasins. (fais/fait/font): **font**

1. Elle … à Nantes. (va/vais/vont)
2. Nous … un gros livre d'histoire. (trouves/trouve/trouvons)
3. Tu … le long de la rue Grimaldi. (continue/continues/continuez)
4. Vous … à droite après le cinéma. (tournes/tournez/tournons)
5. Je … à la maison de la presse. (vais/va/vas)
6. Nous … des recherches. (faites/faisons/fait)
7. Vous … des informations? (trouves/trouvent/trouvez)
8. Tu … des photos. (prends/prend/prennent)
9. On … la place Napoléon. (traversent/traversons/traverse)
10. Tu … le journal régional. (lisez/lisons/lis)

Time to spare? Now give the infinitives of the verbs in the sentences below, for example:

Elles **font** les magasins: **faire**

11. On **choisit** le roman policier.
12. Vous **allumez** la télévision.
13. Philippe **demande** un plan.
14. Il **entre** dans l'office de tourisme.
15. Nous **finissons** le petit-déjeuner.
16. Des touristes **arrivent** à la rivière.
17. Marie-Claude **pose** des questions.
18. Maman **écrit** une liste.
19. Les deux filles **font** du shopping.
20. Tu **écoutes** la radio ce matin.

Exercice 2.10

Now, a chance to revise the futur proche.

Remember that we form the futur proche by using parts of aller, then an **infinitive**. Use the **infinitives** you listed in Exercice 2.9 to help you with this exercise, for example:

Ella **mange** au restaurant.	She **eats** at the restaurant.
Ella **va manger** au restaurant.	She is **going to eat** at the restaurant.
Elle ne **mange** pas.	She **does not eat**.
Elle ne **va** pas **manger**.	She **is not going to eat**.

1. Tu **cherches** des informations.
2. Maman **attend** à la maison avec papa.
3. Chloé **lit** les instructions à la bibliothèque.
4. Magali ne **prend** pas de photos.
5. Elles **vont** à l'université en tramway.
6. Tochiko **retrouve** ses amis à l'office de tourisme.
7. Chloé et Magali **trouvent** l'histoire intéressante.
8. Le frère de Tochiko ne **vient** pas à Nantes.
9. Magali **est** fatiguée.
10. On **mange** au McDo.

Exercice 2.11

Guessing game

What do you think is being described in each definition? Even if you answer first in English, give your answer in French as well, starting:

C'est un(e) …

or, in the plural:

Ce sont des …

1. On peut manger ici mais ce n'est pas un restaurant.
2. Ici, il y a beaucoup d'étudiants et d'étudiantes.
3. C'est une forme de transport public pour aller en ville mais ce n'est pas un bus.
4. Ce sont des images qu'on regarde sur un smartphone.
5. Ici, on peut lire des livres, mais on ne peut pas les acheter.
6. On peut faire de la natation ici.
7. Toutes les semaines, on passe un nouveau film ici.
8. Tous les jours, on achète du pain frais ici.
9. Les personnes qui visitent une ville viennent ici pour trouver des informations.
10. C'est ici qu'on prend le train.

Exercice 2.12

Draw a plan of your ideal town centre, labelling it in French. Use any or all of these words:

un cinéma	a cinema
une boulangerie	a baker's
un bureau de poste	a post office
une maison de la presse	a newsagent's
un café	a café
un restaurant	a restaurant
une rivière et un pont	a river and a bridge
un rond-point	a roundabout
un carrefour	a crossroads
la mairie	the town hall
une bibliothèque	a library
une librairie	a bookshop
un magasin de jouets	a toy shop
une supérette	a small supermarket
une gare SNCF	a train station
un arrêt de tramway	a tram stop
un office de tourisme	a tourist office
un étang	a pond
des champs	fields
des arbres	trees
une ferme	a farm
un parc	a park
un château	a château (anything from a large country house to a castle)

Finally ...

In France, streets, squares, avenues and parks are nearly always named after famous people, events or dates. Why not name your streets after people you admire, to make the town you have invented really special? Use French words for 'street', and so on, then make your hero immortal by adding your choice of name, for example:

rue	Street	e.g. rue Cristiano-Ronaldo
avenue	Avenue	e.g. avenue du Prince-Rainier-de-Monaco
boulevard	Boulevard (long, wide street)	e.g. boulevard François-1er
place	Square	e.g. place François-Hollande

Exercice 2.13

Role play: Au centre-ville (1)

Work in pairs. Take it in turns to be A and B. Say in French:

A. Hello! How do I get to the cinema, please?

B. Bonjour. Quel cinéma?

A. The Belle Épine.

B. Prenez à droite ici. C'est à 200 mètres.

A. There is a good film today.

B. Ah bon? C'est quel genre de film?

A. [Answer the question.]

B. Je n'aime pas. Ce n'est pas mon genre.

A. Is there a café near here?

B. Oui, en face du cinéma.

A. Thank you. Goodbye.

B. De rien. Au revoir.

Exercice 2.14

Role play: Au centre-ville (2)

Work in pairs. Take it in turns to be A and B. B begins.

B. Bonjour, pour aller au stade, s'il vous plaît?

A. I am not from here ...

B. Ah, excusez-moi.

A. ... but I think it is nearby.*

B. Vous n'êtes pas français(e)?

A. No, I'm [e.g. English].

B. Vous parlez bien français!

A. Thank you. Continue for 300 metres.

B. D'accord ... et après?

A. I think it is on the left.

B. Merci beaucoup!

A. You're welcome, goodbye.

B. Au revoir.

* nearby près d'ici

Attention aux faux amis! – Beware of false friends!

Un faux ami is a word or phrase that looks as though it means the same as in English, but turns out to mean something completely different! In this chapter, you will have noticed that une librairie does not mean 'a library' and that there are two terms for the town hall – la mairie and l'hôtel de ville. You'd be a bit disappointed to wander into l'hôtel de ville hoping to book a room!

Why not make your own list of these tricky words and phrases as you go through the book – and beyond!

On fait les magasins!

In this chapter, you will learn how to talk about going shopping and look at the passé composé in more detail.

Exercice 3.1

Listen to the audio then select the correct word to complete the sentences below.

Use the following vocabulary to help you understand the passage.

ça y est!	that's it!; there we are!
l'identité (*f.*)	the identity
bien possible	likely
insupportable	unbearable
faire les magasins	to hit the shops, to go shopping
faire du lèche-vitrines	to go window-shopping

1 Magali pense que c'est ... que J-P. L. est Jean-Paul Lévy. (probable/possible/potable)

2 Les amies vont faire les ... (machines/magazines/magasins)

3 Il est ... (2 h 45/12 h 45/14 h 45)

Exercice 3.2

Listen to the audio again and answer these questions in English.

1 What does Magali initially not understand?
2 How does Tochiko make fun of her?
3 What is the answer that they have found?
4 What is Magali's reaction?
5 What are they going to do now?
6 Why do you think Tochiko says 'parfait!' on being told what time it is?

Exercice 3.3

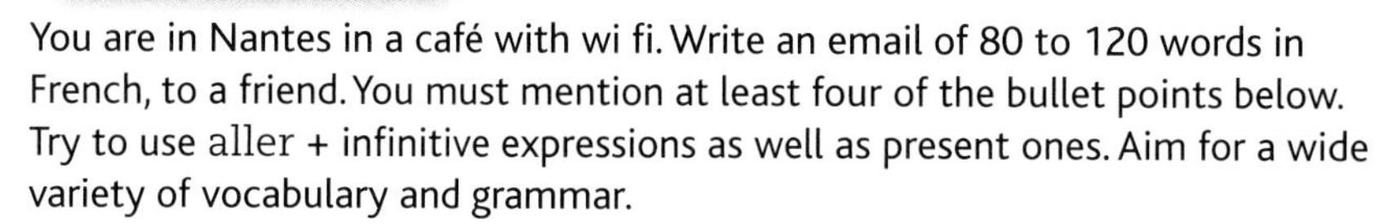

You are in Nantes in a café with wi fi. Write an email of 80 to 120 words in French, to a friend. You must mention at least four of the bullet points below. Try to use aller + infinitive expressions as well as present ones. Aim for a wide variety of vocabulary and grammar.

• coming to Nantes by train	venir à Nantes en train
• the weather	le temps qu'il fait
• where you are	où tu te trouves
• what you are going to do next	ce que tu vas faire maintenant
• what time you are going home	à quelle heure tu vas rentrer

You can also add anything else you want, of course, but you must be pretty sure that what you do use is correct.

Try hard *not* to use language you are unsure of!

Exercice 3.4

La boîte en argent (suite)

Listen to the audio. Use the following vocabulary to help you to understand it. Then choose the correct word to complete each sentence below.

mon chaton	'sweetie', 'darling', etc. (literally my kitten)
en rentrant	on coming home (i.e. when we get back)
on vient de manger	we've just eaten
en arrivant	on arriving
à plus tard!	see you later!
être aux anges	to be over the moon
en train de faire	in the process of doing/making
tu en veux?	do you want some?

1 Quand Chloé appelle, c'est ... qui décroche*. (Magali/maman/papa)

2 Chloé raconte sa journée … (au téléphone/à la maison/dans le train)

3 Chloé va téléphoner en arrivant … (en route/à la gare/à la maison)

4 Maman prépare … (le repas/une boisson/une chambre)

* décrocher — to answer the phone, to pick up

Exercice 3.5

The following passage is split into four parts.

From the choices below, find a heading for each paragraph. One is not needed.

1 Chloé veut acheter des vêtements. Elle demande à Tochiko si, elle aussi, elle veut acheter des vêtements. Tochiko est d'accord. Mais elle veut surtout des souvenirs de Nantes pour sa famille. Magali veut acheter un cadeau pour Mamie.

2 Les filles cherchent un magasin de cadeaux et de souvenirs. Il y en a dans les petites rues près du château. Il y a le tramway, mais ce n'est pas loin. Elles peuvent y aller à pied. Elles trouvent rapidement des petites boutiques intéressantes.

3 Magali demande à Tochiko combien d'argent de poche elle reçoit. Pour Tochiko, cela dépend des petits boulots qu'elle fait pour aider ses parents. Elle range la cuisine après les repas, elle promène le chien et elle fait quelquefois le ménage. Magali lave la voiture de leur mère et Chloé tond la pelouse pour leur père.

4 Chacune des filles reçoit en moyenne dix à quinze euros par semaine. Magali économise, Chloé aime acheter des magazines, Tochiko télécharge beaucoup de musique sur son portable! Elle dépense beaucoup d'argent pour la musique.

un petit boulot	a little job, a task
tondre la pelouse	to mow the lawn
genre (*m.*)	type/sort/style

L'argent de poche	La décision: quel genre de magasin?	
Les petits boulots	Le voyage en train	Les filles partent à pied

Exercice 3.6

Listen to the audio, study the vocabulary, then answer the questions that follow.

il faut (faire) — it is necessary (to do)
un porte-clés — a key ring
une casquette — a cap
un flacon de parfum — a flask of perfume
celui-ci — this one (*m.*)
celui-là — that one (*m.*)
dessus — on it, on top
le/la voisin(e) — the neighbour (*m./f.*)
de temps en temps — from time to time, occasionally
composter un billet — to validate a ticket (get it stamped in a machine)
se dépêcher — to hurry up

1 What would Magali prefer to buy first?
2 What is Tochiko going to buy for her brothers and sisters?
3 What picture is on the T-shirt in front of the one Chloé asks about?
4 How much is the one she wants?

Exercice 3.7

This is an exercise to help you practise speaking. Try miming an action (like the ones listed below) and asking others what they think you are doing. The best entertainment is provided when the mime is not all that good! For example:

A. Qu'est-ce que je fais?

B. Tu … tu ranges ta chambre!

A. Non! Je téléphone!

Here are some more activities to mime:

monter à cheval
faire du ski
faire la cuisine
acheter un souvenir
choisir et lire un livre
se lever
jouer aux boules

Les adverbes – Adverbs

Telling us *how* or *when* things are done

1 Often-used adverbs

You have already met several often-used adverbs:

bien	well	trop	too (much)
vite	quickly	souvent	often
mal	badly	quelquefois	sometimes
mieux	better	longtemps	for a long time
peu	little, not much	déjà	already
pire	worse	toujours	always
encore	again	tous les jours	every day

2 Adverbs ending in -ment

However, you will see many adverbs formed by adding **-ment** to an adjective, rather like adding *-ly* to an adjective in English:

vrai	true	vrai**ment**	truly, really
facile	easy	facile**ment**	easily

There needs to be a vowel before -ment, so if there isn't, the adjective is made **feminine**:

lent	slow	lent**e**ment	slowly
doux	soft	douc**e**ment	softly

To show you have understood, complete these sentences with an adverb to go with the adjective in the first half, for example:

the bicycle is **slow**: it goes **slowly**

1 ma voiture est **lente**: elle roule …
2 sa voix est **douce**: il parle …
3 le train est **rapide**: les passagers voyagent …
4 cet exercice est **facile**: on le fait …
5 la machine est **efficace***: elle fonctionne …

* efficace effective/efficient

Exercice 3.8

Focus on the text! You need to think carefully to match up the sentence halves.

1	**Quand j'arrive au magasin**	(a)	ouvre le magasin de souvenirs?
2	Quand papa est fatigué	(b)	qu'elle choisit à la bibliothèque.
3	Je ne regarde pas la télévision	(c)	**je regarde les T-shirts et les autres souvenirs.**
4	Elle lit le livre	(d)	Chloé va écrire en anglais.
5	Pourquoi n'ouvres-tu pas	(e)	quand j'ai mal aux yeux.
6	Peter va écrire en français et	(f)	au mois de juillet?
7	À l'office de tourisme	(g)	ne sont pas disponibles*.
8	Les informations que je veux	(h)	le cadeau que je te donne?
9	Quel temps fait-il en Italie	(i)	je demande un dépliant sur la ville.
10	À quelle heure	(j)	il ne veut pas discuter avec moi.

* disponible available

Exercice 3.9

La boîte en argent (suite)

Listen as you read, then look at the vocabulary and do the exercise below.

Papa.	Chloé vient de téléphoner. Elles sont sur le point d'arriver à la gare.
Maman.	Tu vas aller les chercher?
Papa.	Bien sûr! Tu viens avec moi?
Maman.	Non. Je reste ici.
Papa.	N'oublie pas que c'est moi qui fais la cuisine ce soir!
Maman.	Ne t'inquiète pas!

* * *

Chloé.	Salut, maman!
Maman.	Mais … où est Tochiko?
Magali.	Son père va la chercher à la gare.
Maman.	Oh, quel dommage! Elle ne va pas dîner chez nous.
Magali.	Je crois que c'est l'anniversaire de sa mère.
Papa.	Alors, quelles sont les nouvelles?

Chloé.	Je crois qu'on connaît le propriétaire de la petite boîte.
Maman.	Mais c'est incroyable! C'est qui?
Magali.	C'est un déporté du village, qui s'appelle Jean-Paul Lévy. Il y a une liste. C'est le seul «J-P. L.»
Maman.	C'est possible, mais il doit être mort.
Chloé.	Mais il doit avoir de la famille. Albertine?
Magali.	Oui! C'est peut-être la femme de Jean-Paul!
Maman.	C'est bien possible …
Papa.	Ou sa sœur?
Maman.	Comment est-ce qu'on va savoir?

il/elle vient de (+ *infin.*)	he/she has just …
sur le point d'arriver	about to arrive
ne t'inquiète pas!	don't worry
quel dommage!	what a shame!; what a pity!
incroyable	incredible
c'est qui?	who is it?
de la famille	some relatives

1 Work in groups. Prepare and perform the conversations above in class.

2 Answer in English:

(a) How does papa know Chloé and Magali need picking up?

(b) What has maman remembered?

(c) Why is Tochiko not able to have supper with Magali and Chloé?

(d) Who do *you* think Albertine might be?

Exercice 3.10

Use the vocabulary provided to help you translate these sentences.

1 I get up, I go downstairs and I make my breakfast.	se lever, descendre, préparer, petit-déjeuner (*m.*)
2 I have cereal, orange juice and coffee.	prendre, céréales (*f.pl.*), jus d'orange (*m.*), café (m.)
3 When I leave the house, it's 8 a.m.	quitter, maison (*f.*), heures (*f.pl.*)
4 I am going to the train station on foot, because it's a nice day.	aller, gare (*f.*), à pied, faire beau
5 At the station, I buy a ticket that I validate.	acheter, billet (*m.*), que, composter.

Exercice 3.11

Write an email in French to a friend, of 80 to 120 words, describing at least **four** of the following. Don't forget to use different verb tenses and to show you know a good range of vocabulary and grammar.

● your morning routine	ta routine du matin
● how you go into town	comment tu vas en ville
● which shops you go to	les magasins où tu vas
● what you buy	ce que tu achètes
● a meal in town	un repas en ville

Le passé composé – The perfect tense

The past tenses: a fuller explanation (1)

There is a brief explanation of the passé composé (equivalent to the present perfect tense in English) in *Book One*. Below, this verb tense is explained in greater detail.

Here is a past-tense version of an exchange between two characters from *Book One*.

Mme Demailly. Magali, qu'est-ce que tu **as fait**, en vacances?

Magali. Bien moi, j'**ai nagé** dans la mer, j'**ai fait** de la planche à voile, j'**ai joué** au foot sur la plage, j'**ai grimpé** aux arbres, puis on **a fait** un pique-nique, on **a** aussi **fait** des promenades ...!

Magali is talking about **past events**, using one of the French past tenses.

Can you see how this past tense is formed? Does it have any similarities to the way we can make a past tense in English?

How to spot past tense expressions

Past tenses usually look and sound similar to these examples:

j'ai nagé	I have swum (using j'ai just like 'I have') *or* I swam
il a chanté	he has sung *or* he sang
vous avez acheté	you have bought *or* you bought

The word coming after the avoir part is called the *past participle*.

Vous avez acheté.

Exercice 3.12

Say whether these expressions are in the present or in the past:

1 j'ai chanté

2 je mange

3 j'ai regardé

4 je trouve

5 j'ai donné

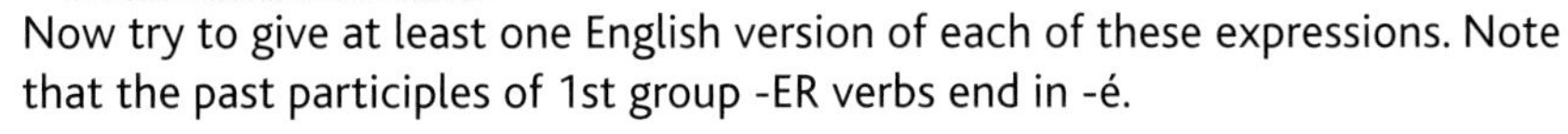

Exercice 3.13

Now try to give at least one English version of each of these expressions. Note that the past participles of 1st group -ER verbs end in -é.

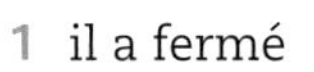

1 il a fermé	(fermer – to close)
2 tu as trouvé	(trouver – to find)
3 il a mangé	(manger – to eat)
4 elle a rangé	(ranger – to tidy)
5 nous avons chanté	(chanter – to sing)
6 vous avez acheté	(acheter – to buy)
7 elles ont joué	(jouer – to play)
8 ils ont bavardé	(bavarder – to chat)
9 tu as marché	(marcher – to walk)
10 on a parlé	(parler – to talk)

Exercice 3.14

Give the right part of avoir for each gap. Again, notice how, after avoir, the second part tells us *what* was done.

1 Magali ... passé les grandes vacances à Dakar.
2 Elle ... fait beaucoup de choses.
3 Chloé ... lu des bandes dessinées.
4 Mme Demailly et Magali ... discuté.
5 Les parents de Magali ... joué au tennis.
6 J'... trouvé une boîte.
7 Vous ... passé deux semaines en Égypte?
8 Oui, nous ... visité les pyramides.
9 Chloé ... fait de la voile?
10 Non, mais elle ... dessiné.

l'Égypte (*f.*)	Egypt
les pyramides (*f. pl.*)	the Pyramids
faire de la voile	to go sailing

Time to spare? Choose five of your answers and say what they mean in English.

Exercice 3.15

Read the sentences below, then answer the questions.

- Magali a parlé à Mme Demailly.
- Nathalie et Jean-Luc ont discuté pendant la pause.
- Marie-Claire a écouté la radio.
- Maman a chanté ce matin.
- Papa et Chloé ont été à Paris.
- J'ai fait mes devoirs et puis j'ai regardé la télévision.
- Magali et Nicole ont pêché des poissons.
- Vous avez écouté les infos*?
- J'ai été malade.

* les infos – abbreviation of les informations the news

1 Who spoke to Mme Demailly?
2 When did Nathalie and Jean-Luc chat?
3 Who sang this morning?
4 What did I do before watching television?
5 What did Magali and Nicole do?

Some unusual past participles

You should now know that j'ai **fait** means 'I have done' or 'I did', so **fait** comes from the verb **faire** ('to do/to make').

J'*ai fait* de la planche à voile.	I *have done* some windsurfing/ I *did* some windsurfing.

Here are a few more odd past participles, from irregular verbs:

Verb		**past participle (after avoir)**	
faire	to do, to make	fait	done, made
avoir	to have	eu	had
être	to be	été	been
lire	to read	lu	read
écrire	to write	écrit	written
prendre	to take	pris	taken

Exercice 3.16

Translate these sentences, using the words given to help you.

You will need to use verbs, after the avoir part, that have the ending -é, as well as été for être and fait for faire.

1 I have been on holiday.	être, vacances (*f.pl*)
2 I have swum in the swimming pool.	nager, piscine (*f.*)
3 I have done some windsurfing.	faire, planche (*f.*) à voile
4 My brother has caught some fish.	pêcher, poisson (*m.*)
5 I have played football at the park.	jouer, foot (*m.*), parc (*m.*)
6 My sisters have bought some nice clothes.	sœur (*f.*), acheter, beau, vêtement (*m.*)

Exercice 3.17

Read the following conversation then do the exercise.

Magali.	J'ai fait des dessins aussi et j'ai pêché.
Mme Demailly.	Tu as attrapé des poissons?
Magali.	Eh oui! Bien sûr!
Mme Demailly.	Et tes parents? Et Chloé?
Magali.	Mes parents ont joué au tennis et Chloé a nagé dans la piscine du camping.
Mme Demailly.	Tes parents ont joué au tennis? Moi aussi j'adore le tennis!
Magali.	Et Chloé a chatté en ligne avec ses amies.
Mme Demailly.	C'est normal, c'est son âge. Qu'est-ce que tu as dessiné?
Magali.	J'ai dessiné des bateaux. J'ai aussi dessiné la voiture de papa.
Mme Demailly.	Regarde. J'ai trouvé ça dans le jardin.
Magali.	Qu'est-ce que c'est?
Mme Demailly.	C'est une vieille boîte en argent!
Magali.	Ça alors!

le camping	the campsite
chatter	to chat online
en ligne	online
un bateau	a boat
bien sûr!	of course!
ça	that (i.e. 'that thing')
une boîte	a box
en argent	(made) of silver
ça alors!	wow!

Complete the sentences with the correct words from the options.

1 Magali ... pêché des poissons. (avez/ont/a)

2 Sa sœur a ... avec ses amies. (chatter/chattez/chatté)

3 Nous avons ... de la planche à voile. (fait/faire/fais)

4 Vous ... été en vacances. (avons/avez/ai)

5 Mme Demailly a ... une boîte. (trouvé/trouver/trouvez)

More about the past tense

We shall be meeting some more irregular (and regular) verbs in this chapter and you will notice that every *past participle* (the correct term for the past tense words that follow *avoir*) is given too.

This will help you recognise more past tense expressions and make sense of the text they appear in.

First of all, let's add the past participles of the remaining irregular verbs we already know.

It is best to **learn** these before moving on!

Verb		**Past participle (after** avoir**)**	
boire	to drink	bu	drunk
courir	to run	couru	run
croire	to believe	cru	believed
devoir	to have to; to owe; must	dû	had to
dire	to say	dit	said
dormir	to sleep	dormi	slept
être	to be	été	been
lire	to read	lu	read
mettre	to put (on)	mis	put
ouvrir	to open	ouvert	opened
pouvoir	to be able to; can	pu	been able
prendre	to take	pris	taken
voir	to see	vu	seen
vouloir	to want	voulu	wanted

Exercice 3.18

Read the text below. Practise and perform it or use it for pronunciation practice.

Maman a invité Mme Demailly à prendre un café après le déjeuner.

Mme Demailly.	Ah. Il est bon, le café.
Maman.	Alors, ton jardin, ça va?
Mme Demailly.	Ah oui. On a eu du beau temps cette année. Vous aussi, en vacances?
Papa.	Ah oui. Au Sénégal, il a fait beau, très beau. Le soleil a brillé tous les jours!
Chloé.	Tous les jours sauf un, papa. Le mercredi au cinéma?
Papa.	Ah oui! Il a plu toute la journée et on a décidé d'aller au cinéma.
Maman.	Et tout le monde a eu la même idée que nous!
Magali.	Oui, on a eu du mal à trouver des places dans la salle!
Chloé.	Et après, on a mangé au restaurant. Quelle histoire!
Mme Demailly.	Pourquoi?
Maman.	Parce que Magali et moi, nous avons choisi tout de suite ...
Magali.	Mais Chloé et papa ont mis du temps à décider! Imaginez ...

le temps	the weather (also 'time', so be aware of the context!)
du beau temps	some fine weather
tous les jours	every day
toute la journée	all day
tout de suite	immediately
il a fait beau	it was fine (weather)
il a plu	it rained; it has rained
même	same
une place	1: a space; 2: a seat (in a cinema, etc.); 3: a town (or village) square
quelle histoire!	what a fiasco!

Exercice 3.19

In this following exercise, simply say which sentences are in the present tense and which are past.

1 Charles entre dans la bibliothèque.
2 Oncle Jules a arrêté sa voiture.
3 Sophie et Marc ont ouvert les volets.
4 Ma mère arrive à cinq heures.
5 Après le concert, nous avons quitté le théâtre.

Quand as-tu fait cela? – When did you do that?

Naturally, 'time' words and phrases make any sentences more interesting. Here are a few that you will come across. They are very common and should be learnt:

hier	yesterday
hier soir	yesterday evening, last night
il y a trois jours	three days ago
la semaine dernière	last week
mardi dernier	last Tuesday
après le film	after the film

La rentrée des classes

It's time to go back to school! In this chapter you'll look at verbs that are followed by infinitives and how to use qui and que.

Exercice 4.1

Read and listen to this passage. The second part is audio only, so you will hear it but not see it printed below, but it carries on from the first that you hear and read.

On est au mois de septembre. Les feuilles ont commencé à changer de couleur et quelques-unes sont déjà tombées des arbres. Pourtant, il fait beau et assez chaud. Il n'y a pas de vent, mais le soleil a perdu sa force et on sent venir l'automne. C'est la rentrée des classes.
Magali et Chloé viennent de retourner à la maison après de longues vacances au bord de la mer. Elles se sont bien amusées, mais elles se sont aussi reposées.

Les filles ont découvert beaucoup de choses intéressantes. Elles ont finalement trouvé le nom du mystérieux «J-P. L.», le propriétaire de la boîte en argent dans le jardin de leur voisine, Madame Demailly. Chloé est quand même impatiente de retrouver ses copains et copines en rentrant au collège.

la feuille	the leaf
tomber	to fall
perdre	to lose
la force	strength, power
sentir (*irregular*)	to feel, to sense
se reposer	to rest
retrouver (quelqu'un)	to meet up (with someone)
la Nouvelle-Orléans	New Orleans
fanatique (de)	very keen (on)
on dirait que ...	it looks like ...

ça se voit	it's obvious
le tien, la tienne	yours
changer de …	to change (something)
se passer	to happen

Keep listening, then complete the sentences.

1 L'histoire se passe en … (hiver/automne/été)

2 Madame Demailly est la … de Chloé. (voisine/voisin/voisinage)

3 Le soleil est … (fort/faible/dur)

4 La Nouvelle-Orléans se trouve en … (Amérique/Afrique/Europe)

5 Chloé est dans la ... de Sabine. (école/maison/classe)

Verbs followed by infinitives

On sent venir l'automne. One can sense autumn coming.

The first verb is *conjugated* (in other words, you use the person and tense that are appropriate) and the second verb is *infinitive* and does not change. Here are some more examples:

aller chercher	to go and get/fetch
faire faire	to have (something) done or made
faire venir	to get (someone) to come, to send for
laisser faire	to let (someone) do as they please
laisser tomber	to drop
venir chercher	to come and get
Il laisse tomber le livre.	He drops the book.
On a fait faire un mur.	We had a wall made.
J'ai fait venir le médecin.	I sent for the doctor.
Paul joue mal, mais je le laisse faire.	Paul plays badly, but I let him get on with it.

Exercice 4.2

Translate the following phrases.

Important! Use your answers to Exercice 4.3 to help you. Remember that, when writing French, you should not just translate word for word, and you should always ask yourself what **tense** a verb should be in.

1 it is October

2 some (*f.*) are already leaving

3 Jean and Sabine have just phoned

4 we (on) are going to do interesting things

5 the owner of the bike

Exercice 4.3

Use the vocabulary here and above to help you translate these sentences:

1 My sister drops the vase.	laisser tomber, vase (*m.*)
2 Paul's neighbour sends for the doctor.	voisine (*f.*), faire venir, médecin (*m.*)
3 You (*sing.*) have a greenhouse made.	faire faire, serre (*f.*)
4 I let my little brother play.	laisser jouer, petit, frère (*m.*)
5 Chloé comes to get her sister.	venir chercher, sœur (*f.*)

Exercice 4.4

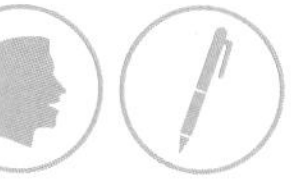

Find the French for these phrases in Exercice 4.1.

1 it is September

2 some (*f.*) are already falling

3 Magali and Chloé have just returned

4 they (*f.*) did lots of interesting things

5 the owner of the box

Exercice 4.5

97

Listen to the audio then complete the sentences below the vocabulary.

afficher	to put up, to post
le couloir	the corridor
la fête	the party
le casier	the locker

1 Magali ne sait pas où aller, parce qu'elle n'a pas … l'affiche.

2 À côté des casiers, il y a les … de classes.

3 La … est ce soir.

4 … ne peut pas venir à la fête.

5 Elle dit qu'elle doit demander à sa …

Exercice 4.6

This is an email sent by Tochiko to her sister Mina. Read it and do the exercise below.

> **De:** tochiko@ ...
>
> **À:** mina@ ...
>
> **Objet:** Salut
>
> Salut Mina
>
> Je suis au collège. Ça va, mais tout est nouveau. Je suis en sixième avec Madame Meunier. Elle est assez sympa mais elle est prof d'histoire-géo et je trouve ça difficile. J'ai un problème. On m'a invitée à une fête ce soir pour l'anniversaire de Chloé, mais je ne veux pas y aller parce qu'on nous a donné des tas de devoirs et je veux travailler cette année. Il faut absolument que je trouve une excuse! Aide-moi! Réponds-moi vite!
>
> Bises
>
> Toch

des tas de (*spoken language*)	masses of/lots of
absolument	absolutely

Supply the missing words in this passage with words from the box below. The first has been done. Two of the words in the box will not be needed.

Tochiko ... **est** ... à l'école quand elle ... un e-mail à Mina. Elle ... Madame Meunier, mais elle n'aime pas ... l'histoire-géo. Elle trouve ce sujet .... Tochiko veut ... ses ..., donc elle demande à Mina de ... une excuse.

trouver	envoie	difficile
aime	devoirs	faire
beaucoup	trouves	aimer

Exercice 4.7

Compose Mina's reply to her sister. Write 30–50 words.

Here are some words and phrases to help you:

tu peux dire que ...	you can say that ...
dis-lui que ...	tell her that ...
tu dois ...	you have to ...
la vérité	the truth
ou	or
ou bien	or perhaps
toujours	always

Exercice 4.8

Role play: Arrangements to go out ... or not

Work in pairs. Take it in turns to be A and B. It is a phone conversation.

A. Hello?*

B. Salut Henri, c'est Paul. Tu veux venir au cinéma ce soir?

A. I can't. [Give an excuse.]

B. Ah mince. Et mercredi?

A. It's my brother's birthday.

B. Ah oui. J'ai un cadeau pour lui.

A. That's kind. What is it?

B. Un T-shirt du Tour de France.

A. That's great. He loves cycling.
Where did you buy the present?

B. À Pau, en vacances ...

* Allô, not bonjour!

Exercice 4.9

Au collège, il y a un club de correspondance internationale organisé par un professeur. Chloé a un correspondant anglais, Peter, mais Tochiko et Philippe n'ont pas de correspondants. Philippe regarde les petites annonces dans le journal du club. Philippe aime faire la fête, faire des randonnées en montagne, jouer au basketball, écouter du rap à la radio et faire du vélo. Tochiko adore la musique classique, aller à la plage, manger de la nourriture orientale et elle aime aussi les romans policiers.

une petite annonce	a small ad
la nourriture	food
oriental	oriental
idéal (*m.pl.* idéaux)	ideal

Look at the adverts. Who would be the best correspondents for Philippe and Tochiko, and why?

Club de correspondance internationale		
Prénom	Joshua	Mireille
Nationalité	anglaise	suisse
Âge	13 ans	12 ans
Aime	le football	la danse
	les voitures de sport	le sport
	Mozart	le cyclisme
N'aime pas	la campagne	la musique ancienne
Prénom	Claudia	Mark
Nationalité	allemande	américaine
Âge	12 ans	13 ans
Aime	les promenades	la cuisine japonaise
	le jazz	la musique du 19e siècle
	la lecture	la lecture
N'aime pas	le sport	les bandes dessinées

Exercice 4.10

Now write one advert for yourself and one for a friend.

Prénom	
Nationalité	
Âge	
Aime	
N'aime pas	

A question for the curious among you:

Why is the nationality of everyone in the club de correspondance ads given in the feminine?

Qui and que

You will have noticed that qui and que have more than one meaning. When they are question words, they are always the same: qui? means 'who?' and que? means 'what?'. However, they have other functions. Here are some examples:

1 **Question words**

qui?	who?
Qui est à l'appareil?	Who is on the phone?
que?	what?
Que fais-tu?	What are you doing?

2 **Relative pronouns**

qui	who, which, that (with the verb as next word)

This is your chance to work out the English for yourself!

la jeune fille qui écrit la lettre	the girl ... writes the letter
le vase qui est sur la table	the vase ... is on the table
la chose qui inquiète mon père	the thing ... worries my father
que (or qu')*	who, which, that (separated from the verb)
le garçon que tu as vu	the boy ... you saw
le vase qu'il a brisé	the vase ... he broke
la maison qu'elle va acheter	the house ... she is going to buy

*Don't forget that qui is never shortened, but que becomes qu' before a vowel or silent 'h'.

3 **'That' as in 'it's true *that* I am French'**

que	that
Je sais que tu veux partir	I know that you want to leave

Reminder: You that, while you can sometimes leave out these words in English – 'the boy (who) you saw', 'I know (that) you want to leave' – you can *never* omit them in French.

When you are working out whether to use qui or que, if you can leave it out in English then it is que in French.

Exercice 4.11

Recopie ces phrases, avec *qui*, *que* ou *qu'*:

1 C'est moi ... ai écrit la lettre.

2 ... est dans ma classe cette année?

3 Tochiko n'aime pas les enfants ... se plaignent* tout le temps.

4 ... a lu le nouveau '*Harry Potter*'?

5 C'est un roman ... tout le monde aime énormément.

6 ... est le Président de la République?

7 ... est-ce qu'on va manger ce soir?

8 On va manger l'escalope ... tu as choisie hier.

9 Le film ... tu regardes est effrayant.

10 C'est ma mère ... va faire la cuisine.

Pour aller plus loin ...

11 Où sont les cahiers ... elle cherche?

12 Le livre ... il veut lire est excellent.

13 Les repas ... on sert au collège sont assez bons.

14 Le prof ... parle en ce moment s'appelle M. Béchet.

15 Où as-tu mis le magazine ... je veux lire?

* se plaindre (*irregular*)	to complain
un roman	a novel
énorme	huge
énormément	enormously, very much
une escalope	an escalope/a thin steak
effrayant	scary, frightening

Exercice 4.12

Compose an email in French describing your first day back at school (la rentrée des classes dans ton école) in September. Write 80–120 words. You must mention the following four points:

• a new friend	un nouvel ami/une nouvelle amie
• the food at school	la nourriture à l'école
• the subjects you are going to do this year	les matières que tu vas faire cette année
• what you did this morning	ce que tu as fait ce matin

Exercice 4.13

ce que tu as fait	what you did, what you have done
pas terrible	not great
ne t'en fais pas	don't worry about it

Listen to the audio. Answer the questions in English.

1 What lessons does Philippe have this afternoon?
2 What is Tochiko's opinion of Spanish?
3 Why does Magali not know which lessons she has?
4 Where do you think salade niçoise and pâtes à la napolitaine had their origins?
5 Why does Tochiko say she cannot go to the party?
6 What is Chloé's reaction?

Speaking on a prepared topic

A prepared talk is used in some exams as a way of encouraging you to talk relatively freely. It is always useful to be able to say a few things about yourself, to get a proper conversation going and to help you find out more about the person you are talking to. You need to express your opinions – about anything! – and say why you have them.

In this chapter, we shall continue the school theme and prepare some basic things to say. In the following chapters, you will be invited to give information and opinions on the main topic and, in this way, you will build up your ability to speak on a whole range of things.

But how do we turn a prepared talk into a conversation? You could just go through the entire school day, giving the times at which you do absolutely everything, but this would not be very interesting to listen to! It is much better to say that you arrive in class at a certain time, that you have a certain number of lessons a day, that you particularly like a certain subject, why (giving an interesting reason) and that you are not keen on something else (giving a polite reason!). You could say something interesting about your school, whether you find the work hard or easy, whether the food is good or bad. Finally, *listen* to the examiner's questions. Be prepared to answer them, as this will turn a talk into a conversation.

In the next exercise, we look at a possible way to structure your talk.

Exercice 4.14

Prepared talk: Life and work at school

In this exercise, you have to prepare to say in French a few things about your life and work at school. Use the following as a guide.

- D'habitude j'arrive en classe à [huit heures et quart].
- Dans ma classe, nous sommes [dix-sept].
- Le matin, avant le déjeuner, on a [cinq] cours.
- On mange [bien] à la cantine.
- Aujourd'hui, on est [jeudi]. J'aime les [jeudis] mais je préfère les [lundis] parce que nous avons [latin] et j'adore ça.
- Aujourd'hui, on a [anglais] et je n'aime pas beaucoup ça parce que [le prof est sévère].
- Les cours finissent à [dix-sept heures] et je rentre à la maison [en bus].

Now *learn* what you have prepared. You won't be allowed notes in the exam.

Exercice 4.15

Role play: A conversation at school

You (A) are in an histoire-géo lesson in a French school with a friend (B). Take it in turns to be A and B.

A. What time does the lesson end?

B. Dans deux minutes normalement*.

A. Is it lunchtime?

B. Oui. Tu as faim?

A. No, I want to phone my parents.

B. On mange à la cantine après?

A. Yes, at about 12 h 30.

B. Ça marche.
Qu'est-ce que tu aimes manger?

A. [Answer the question.]

B. Moi aussi.

A. History lessons are different in the UK.

B. Ça ne m'étonne pas!

* normalement usually

La vie de tous les jours: le travail et les loisirs

In this chapter, you'll look at the topic of work and free time and learn about verbs that use être instead of avoir in the passé composé.

Exercice 5.1

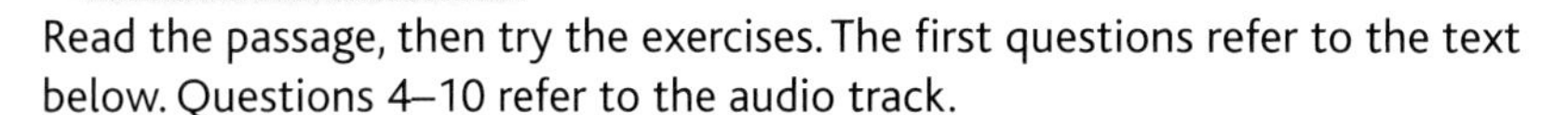
Read the passage, then try the exercises. The first questions refer to the text below. Questions 4–10 refer to the audio track.

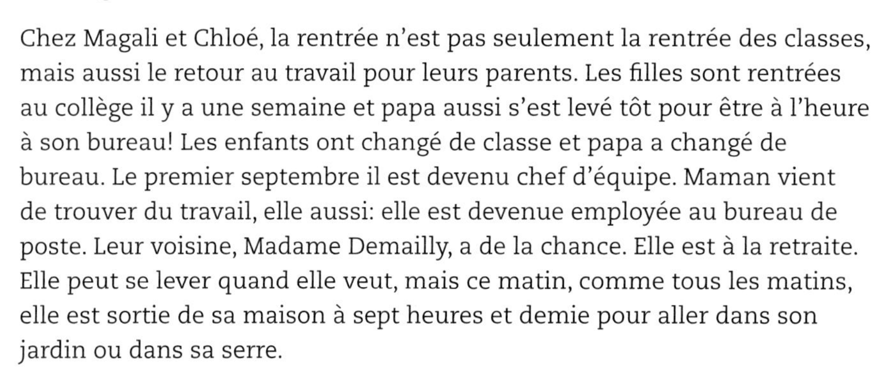
Chez Magali et Chloé, la rentrée n'est pas seulement la rentrée des classes, mais aussi le retour au travail pour leurs parents. Les filles sont rentrées au collège il y a une semaine et papa aussi s'est levé tôt pour être à l'heure à son bureau! Les enfants ont changé de classe et papa a changé de bureau. Le premier septembre il est devenu chef d'équipe. Maman vient de trouver du travail, elle aussi: elle est devenue employée au bureau de poste. Leur voisine, Madame Demailly, a de la chance. Elle est à la retraite. Elle peut se lever quand elle veut, mais ce matin, comme tous les matins, elle est sortie de sa maison à sept heures et demie pour aller dans son jardin ou dans sa serre.

tôt	early
changer (de ...)	to change (something)
devenir	to become
le chef d'équipe	team leader
la serre	greenhouse
rédiger	to write
de bonne heure	early
la revue	magazine, newsletter
à temps	on time
mensuel	monthly
le plaisir	pleasure
se donner de la peine	to make an effort, to go to trouble
faire la grasse matinée	to have a lie-in

Answer the questions in English.

Reading passage

1 When did Magali and Chloé go back to school?

2 Why has papa changed offices?

3 Why can Mme Demailly decide for herself what time she gets up in the morning?

Audio

4 When does Mme Demailly get up at 7 o'clock?

5 Why is she able to get up early?

6 What does she do in the evening apart from reading the newspaper?

7 What is her opinion of what is on television?

8 What must she do for the gardening club?

9 Why is papa not seen before noon at the weekend?

10 What does Magali do?

Verbs using être in the passé composé

Some verbs use être in the passé composé instead of avoir.

Did you notice these expressions in the text above?

les filles sont rentrées	the girls went back (to school)
papa s'est levé	papa got up
il est devenu	he has become
elle est devenue	she has become

Some French verbs make their past tense with être instead of avoir. The important thing, as always, is to listen for the second word, which tells you what was done, for example you know aller means 'to go', so je suis allé means 'I went' or 'I have gone'. One more thing: in verbs conjugated with être, the past participle has to agree with the subject. So if the je of je suis allé is feminine, it becomes je suis allée. If the subject is plural, ils sont allés or elles sont allées.

The verbs conjugated with être are best arranged in pairs. Can you say what the connection is in each pair and what most of these verbs have in common?

aller	to go	venir	to come
entrer	to go in	sortir	to go out
arriver	to arrive	partir	to leave (depart)
monter	to go up	descendre	to go down
tomber	to fall	rester	to stay
naître	to be born	mourir	to die
rentrer	to go home, to go/come back in	retourner	to turn back, to return

Exercice 5.2

Translate:

1	Papa went to bed after me.	aller, lit (*m.*)
2	My grandfather fell in the garden.	tomber, jardin (*m.*)
3	He went out to walk the dog.	sortir, promener, chien (*m.*)
4	Philippe came to the party.	venir (*pp.* venu), fête (*f.*)
5	You (*m.sing.*) went home at 3 p.m.	rentrer, maison (*f.*)

Pour aller plus loin ...

6	My father left first.	(say: ... *the* first), partir, premier
7	He arrived before the others.	arriver, autres (*m. pl.*)
8	Marc's brother stayed in Paris.	frère (*m.*), rester
9	Charles's friend came downstairs.	ami (*m.*), descendre
10	The King died in 1952.	roi *(m.),* mourir (*pp.* mort)

Exercice 5.3

Vrai ou faux?

Read this passage then decide whether the statements below are true or false.

Au collège, les cours finissent à dix-sept heures trente, c'est-à-dire à cinq heures et demie du soir. Il y a un bus à 17 h 45, alors, au lieu de rentrer tout de suite à la maison, Magali a bavardé avec quelques amies dans le préau et Chloé a passé le temps à feuilleter un magazine. Lorsqu'elles sont arrivées chez elles, Chloé a pris la clé dans son cartable et a ouvert la porte d'entrée. Elle n'a trouvé personne, parce que maman rentre à 18 h 30 et papa arrive d'habitude un peu après. Donc c'est Magali qui a donné à manger au chat et Chloé qui a mis la table pour le repas du soir. Le chat est toujours très content de revoir les jeunes. Il a ronronné de plaisir en mangeant son dîner. Magali sait que le chat adore le lait et lui en a versé un peu dans une soucoupe.

préau (*m.*)	covered playground
feuilleter	to flick through
revoir	to see again
la soucoupe	saucer
ronronner	to purr
verser	to pour

1 À l'école, les classes se terminent avant seize heures.

2 Après les classes, Magali et Chloé sont rentrées immédiatement à la maison.

3 Magali a parlé avec ses copines et Chloé a lu.

4 Maman a ouvert la porte quand les filles sont arrivées.

5 Papa rentre à la maison avant maman.

6 Le soir, à la maison, la sœur de Chloé s'est occupée du chat.

Exercice 5.4

Listen to the audio. The vocabulary below must be learnt.

le guichet	the till, the counter*
faire le tour (de ...)	to go around (something)
la montre	wristwatch
la pendule	clock (*on the wall*)
ne t'en fais pas	don't worry
la boîte aux lettres	letter box
la balance	weighing scales
tomber en panne	to break down
donner un coup de main	to give a (helping) hand
le merlan	whiting (*fish*)

* The word guichet can mean 'ticket office' or 'box office', but it is also used for the glass-fronted counter in a post office or bank.

Answer in English:

1 Why can Chloé not tell Magali what the time is?

2 What does she tell Magali to do?

3 What does Magali think maman has been doing today?

4 Where was she in fact working?

5 What was the first reason that she had had a hard day?

6 Where and when did maman buy the melon?

Exercice 5.5

Match the English expressions to the French. One is done for you: **1 = j**.

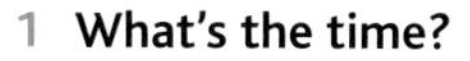

1 **What's the time?**	(a) Quelle journée!
2 The sitting-room clock.	(b) C'est papa qui rentre.
3 Did you hear that?	(c) Tu as entendu ça?
4 It's Dad coming home.	(d) Je l'ai acheté.
5 I'll open the door for her.	(e) Je te donne un coup de main?
6 What a day!	(f) La pendule du salon.
7 You go round the village.	(g) Je vais lui ouvrir.
8 Shall I give you a hand?	(h) Je vais me changer.
9 I'm going to get changed.	(i) Tu fais le tour du village.
10 I bought it.	(j) **Il est quelle heure?**

Exercice 5.6

Prepared talk

This type of exercise is to help you prepare to speak in French for a short time without stopping. Read the instructions through before you begin.

Describe the following situation. Write rough notes in French (don't worry too much about spelling).

1 You arrive home at 5.50 in the evening. There is no one at home. You open the door and go in. Your mum or dad arrives home after you, then your brother. You start to prepare the evening meal.

2 Try telling the same story in the past tense.

Exercice 5.7

Les tâches ménagères – **Household chores**

Listen to the audio. Give the correct French word for each number. Write a list of the numbers first.

Un jour à l'**[1]**, tous les élèves parlent devant la classe des tâches ménagères, c'est-à-dire des petits boulots qu'ils doivent faire pour aider leurs parents à la maison. Les parents de Magali et Chloé travaillent tous les deux, alors tout le monde est obligé de donner un coup de **[2]**. La semaine dernière, par exemple, Chloé a beaucoup aidé à la cuisine et Magali a travaillé dans le jardin. On leur demande ce qu'elles ont fait.

Professeur. Magali, qu'est-ce que tu as fait la semaine dernière, pour [3] tes parents?

Magali. Eh bien, moi, j'ai travaillé dans le jardin. J'ai **[4]** la pelouse, ce qui est assez dur en ce moment car la tondeuse est assez vieille et elle peut tomber en **[5]** d'un moment à l'autre! Puis papa m'a demandé de planter des bulbes au bord de la terrasse. Il a dit que ça allait donner des tulipes au **[6]**. Après cela, j'ai dû creuser des trous pour y planter des têtes d'ail. Pour creuser j'ai utilisé une pelle. J'ai préparé la terre pour les légumes avec une fourche, j'ai arraché les mauvaises herbes et j'ai tout ratissé avec un râteau après avoir planté les graines. Puis j'ai **[7]**, bien sûr.

Professeur. Merci, Magali. On voit que tu aimes le jardinage!

Magali. Ah oui. J'adore ça.

Professeur. Et toi, Chloé. Qu'as-tu fait?

Chloé.	Quant à moi, j'ai surtout aidé à la cuisine, car on arrive d'habitude le soir avant maman et papa. La semaine [8], j'ai mis la table tous les soirs et lundi j'ai aidé à préparer le repas. D'abord, j'ai dû éplucher les pommes de terre et les mettre dans une grande casserole, puis j'ai [9] de l'eau et du sel. Ça fait du bruit quand on ouvre le robinet pour faire couler l'eau froide, et puis on a du mal à le refermer! J'ai allumé le gaz et j'ai mis la casserole sur la cuisinière. Après le repas, Magali a [10] la table et elle a fait la vaisselle, mais c'est maman qui a tout rangé dans les placards.
Professeur.	Et tu fais autre chose, pour aider à la maison?
Chloé.	Oui. Je nettoie la voiture. J'aime ça!

le bulbe	bulb (e.g. of a tulip)
la tulipe	tulip
la terrasse	terrace, patio
creuser	to dig
le trou	hole
la tête d'ail	garlic bulb
la pelle	spade
la fourche	fork
arracher	to pull up (e.g. a garden weed)
la mauvaise herbe	weed
ratisser	to rake
le râteau	rake
planter	to plant
la graine	seed

arroser	to water
éplucher	to peel
la casserole	saucepan
ajouter	to add
le robinet	tap
ouvrir un robinet	to turn on a tap
fermer un robinet	to turn off a tap
couler	to flow
refermer	to turn off again, to close again
la cuisinière	cooker
débarrasser la table	to clear the table
le placard	cupboard
autre chose	something else

Exercice 5.8

Learn the vocabulary given with Exercice 5.7 a few words at a time. Your teacher will test you on them.

Exercice 5.9

Write a short paragraph (or a few sentences) about what you do to help at home and what your brothers and sisters do.

Exercice 5.10

Tochiko receives an email from Mireille, a Belgian friend. Copy the text, filling in the blank spaces with words from the box below. Note that two are not necessary!

De: mireille.poirot@ …

Objet: Salut

À: tochiko@ …

Salut Tochiko

Ça fait une heure et demie que je suis dans ma chambre. Je m'ennuie, parce que j'ai fini mes … et je n'ai pas de bon livre à …. Il pleut et je … le mauvais …. Hier, j'ai dû aider mon père à la …. On a préparé des filets de … et de la salade. Je n'aime pas faire la cuisine, je … travailler … le jardin.

Réponds-moi vite! Je t'embrasse,

Mireille

dans	déteste	cuisine	poisson	temps
devoirs	préfère	lire	frère	préféré

Exercice 5.11

Vrai ou faux – **True or false**

Here's an email that Tochiko wrote *answering* one she had received. Using the vocabulary to help you if necessary, say whether the statements below are true or false (vrai ou faux), according to the message.

De: tochiko@ ...

Objet: Salut

À: mireille.poirot@ ...

Bonjour Mireille

Alors, toi aussi tu es obligée de travailler à la maison! Moi, ça ne me dérange pas. Je dois aider papa avec le jardinage, mais j'aime ça. Oui, le dimanche, je fais des petits boulots: je débarrasse la table et je sors les poubelles. Non, je ne m'ennuie pas. Je reçois vingt euros par semaine. Ici, aujourd'hui, il fait beau. Hier, comme chez toi, il a fait froid.

Non, le soir je fais mes devoirs dans ma chambre, pas devant la télé: j'ai du mal à me concentrer. Mes parents vont bien, merci. J'espère que tu peux réparer ton vélo. Oui, j'adore le cyclisme.

À bientôt!

Tochiko

être obligé de (+ *infin.*)	to have to/to be obliged to
ça ne me dérange pas	I don't mind that
les petits boulots	chores
avoir du mal à (+ *infin.*)	to find it hard to

1 Tochiko has to do some work to help at home.

2 She objects to doing chores.

3 Tochiko lays the table for Sunday lunch.

4 It was cold yesterday.

5 She does her homework in front of the television.

Exercice 5.12

Une conversation téléphonique

Listen to the conversation while reading it.

Mina. Ciao*, Tochiko!

Tochiko. Alors, tu parles italien maintenant?

Mina. Oui, un mot! Pourquoi tu m'appelles?

Tochiko. Où es-tu?

Mina. Dans le jardin. Pourquoi?

Tochiko. Qu'est-ce que tu vas faire samedi?

Mina. Comme toi. On va nettoyer le garage, tu te rappelles?

Tochiko. Ah oui. On ne peut pas aller au concert alors.

Mina. Quel concert?

Tochiko. Le concert en plein air de Danny Lefou à La Roche …

Mina. Danny Lefou!!

Tochiko. Oui, mais le garage …

Mina. Pourquoi tu ne m'as rien dit? Danny à La Roche! … Ça commence à quelle heure?

Tochiko. Midi et demi.

Mina. On peut faire le nettoyage après!

Tochiko. J'ai déjà acheté les billets.

Mina. Je te déteste.

Tochiko. Merci. À ce soir, petite sœur.

* ciao! 'hi' (or 'bye') in Italian; used occasionally in French, as in English

The information in the sentences below is wrong. Correct the sentences:

1 Mina est **dans le salon** quand Tochiko téléphone.

2 Les filles ont décidé de **faire leurs devoirs** samedi.

3 Le concert de Danny Lefou va commencer **samedi soir**.

4 Tochiko **n'a pas acheté** les billets.

5 «Ciao» veut dire **«musique»** en italien.

Exercice 5.13

Work in pairs. Make up a phone conversation (or part of one) similar to that in Exercice 5.12. Change the names and details. Prepare and perform it in class.

Exercice 5.14

Below in Section A are extracts of conversations with young people, about chores they do to help at home. Match the statements in Section B to the people in Section A.

Section A

Luc. D'habitude en été, s'il fait beau le mercredi après-midi, je tonds la pelouse pour maman. Nous sommes deux à la maison. Ma mère travaille à la pharmacie à plein temps et le mercredi après-midi je suis libre. Elle me donne vingt euros par semaine. Ça me suffit.

Françoise. Mes parents sont assez généreux. Ils me donnent quinze euros par semaine. Je suis obligée de ranger ma chambre, de mettre la table le matin pour le petit-déjeuner, mais à part ça on ne me demande pas grand-chose.

Marc. J'ai treize ans et je n'aime pas mettre les vêtements démodés ou bon marché que ma mère m'achète, mais je n'ai pas le choix. J'ai proposé de faire le ménage à la maison mais ma mère veut me donner seulement dix euros, donc ce n'est pas intéressant.

Jean-Paul.	Mon père est musicien et moi je m'intéresse aussi beaucoup à la musique. On va ensemble acheter des partitions ou des cordes de violon, donc il comprend bien combien d'argent il me faut. Je ne dépense pas beaucoup: je suis trop radin! À la maison je fais le ménage et je m'occupe des animaux.
Sandrine.	J'ai une amie qui reçoit deux fois plus d'argent de poche que moi, mais elle doit acheter tous ses vêtements et payer son déjeuner à la cantine de l'école. Moi, je dois ranger ma chambre et celle de ma sœur qui a onze ans! Pour ça, on me donne vingt euros.

à plein temps	full time
ça me suffit	it's enough for me
démodé	unfashionable
bon marché	cheap
ensemble	together
la partition	piece of sheet music
la corde	string
le violon	violin
dépenser	to spend (money)
radin	mean

Section B

1 J'aime porter des vêtements chics, mais ils sont chers.

2 Je ne fais pas grand-chose mais mes parents me donnent assez d'argent.

3 Ma mère n'a pas le temps de travailler dans le jardin.

4 Je suis très content parce que mon père a les mêmes intérêts que moi.

5 Ma copine reçoit quarante euros par semaine.

Pour aller plus loin ...

6 Un jour par semaine je rentre de l'école à midi.

7 Je mets les couteaux et les bols sur la table pour toute la famille.

8 Mon père n'habite pas avec nous.

9 Nous avons trois chats et c'est moi qui leur donne à manger.

10 J'ai voulu acheter un beau jean mais ma mère a dit qu'il était beaucoup trop cher.

Exercice 5.15

Écoute Sabine, qui raconte une journée typique. Trouve la photo pour chaque partie.

Écris la lettre de la bonne réponse, comme dans l'exemple:

Je me lève à sept heures.

1 (a)  

(b)  

(c) 

Réponse: c

2 (a)  

(b) 

(c) 

3 (a) 

(b) 

(c) 

4 (a) 

(b) 

(c) 

5 (a) 

(b) 

(c) 

Exercice 5.16

Role play: Daily routine

Take it in turns to be A and B. B starts.

B. Tu te lèves à quelle heure, d'habitude?

A. [Answer the question.]

B. Qu'est-ce que tu manges le matin?

A. I like croissants.

B. Tu bois du thé?

A. Yes, but I prefer chocolate. What time do you go to school?

B. Je pars vers huit heures.

A. How many lessons do you have in the morning?

B. J'ai trois heures et une pause.

A. What do you do to help at home?

B. Je passe l'aspirateur, je range ma chambre ...

Exercice 5.17

Prepared talk: A town or region

Prepare to speak in French for 30 seconds on any town or area that you know in France. If you have not been to France yet, you may find information on the internet. You may even speak about your home town or region.

- Select the place you want to speak about
- Describe where it is geographically
- Describe how it is set out (e.g. lots of little streets and a town square, etc.)
- Say what else is there (activities for tourists, historic sites, etc.)
- Give your opinion of it.

Exercice 5.18

Compose an email in French in which you talk about your daily routine. You must mention at least **four** of the following five points:

• what time you get up	à quelle heure tu te lèves
• a typical breakfast	un petit-déjeuner classique
• your school day	ta journée scolaire
• where you have lunch	où tu prends le déjeuner
• what you are going to do this evening	ce que tu vas faire ce soir

6 On fait un tour en Normandie

In this chapter you'll visit Normandy and take a look at negatives.

Chloé et Magali sont allées en vacances au Sénégal. Mais tout le monde ne fait pas la même chose! Tochiko n'a pas voyagé à l'étranger*. Et pour les vacances de la Toussaint**, elle a passé des vacances un peu différentes. La famille de Tochiko est allée là où le soleil n'a pas brillé tous les jours et il n'a pas fait très chaud!

* à l'étranger	abroad
** vacances de la Toussaint	Autumn half-term holiday

Saying what did not happen

When we say what has **not** happened in the past, we add ne and pas to the part of avoir before putting the past participle:

elle a voyagé	she has travelled/she travelled
elle **n'**a **pas** voyagé	she has not travelled/she didn't travel

Exercice 6.1

Give the English for:

1. il n'a pas trouvé
2. nous n'avons pas écouté
3. vous n'avez pas continué
4. on n'a pas écrit
5. tu n'as pas lu
6. ils n'ont pas parlé
7. je n'ai pas mangé
8. Philippe n'a pas entendu
9. maman n'a pas chanté
10. Jacques et Chloé n'ont pas regardé

Exercice 6.2

Write these sentences in the negative:

1 J'ai regardé la pendule.
2 La pendule a été sur la cheminée.
3 Elle a vu maman.
4 Marie a lu tous les soirs.
5 Elle a ouvert la porte.

Exercice 6.3

Listen to the audio. Try to describe in French the general subject of the passage.

proposer	to suggest
promettre (*like* mettre)	to promise
conduire	to drive (*see below*)
produire	to produce
la ferme-auberge	farmhouse taking paying guests
un fauteuil roulant	wheelchair
louer	to rent, to hire

Exercice 6.4

Listen again. Answer the questions in English.

1 Why has Tochiko never been to a farm?
2 What sort of farm would she like to visit?
3 How much holiday does she have?
4 What will Marie-Christine do at the farm?
5 Why is it difficult to find the right sort of place for the family to stay?

Exercice 6.5

Translate:

1 Tochiko has never visited a farm.	ne … jamais, visiter, ferme (*f.*)
2 It is a farm where they make cheese.	fabriquer, fromage (*m.*)
3 She has two weeks of holiday.	semaine (*f.*), vacances (*f.pl.*)
4 Her mother suggests that they spend the holidays in Normandy.	proposer, Normandie
5 Maman says that she can rent rooms.	dire, pouvoir, louer, chambre (*f.*)

Exercice 6.6

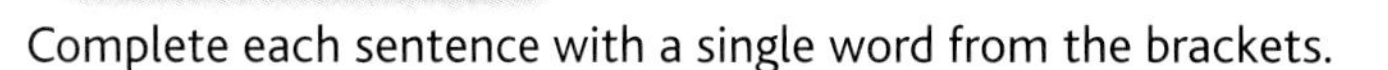

Complete each sentence with a single word from the brackets.

1 Je ne suis ... allé à Paris.	(jamais, rien, personne)
2 Ici, … fait du bon pain.	(ils, nous, on)
3 Je ... qu'on joue au tennis.	(promet, produis, propose)
4 Il … préparer un bon dîner.	(a, est, va)
5 L'amie de … tante n'a jamais vu le château.	(mon, ma, mes)

Pour aller plus loin ...

6 Ils ne … pas louer le chalet.	(peut, peuvent, pouvez)
7 C'est une ville où … fabrique des voitures.	(nous, ils, on)
8 La mer est … une heure de route.	(vers, d', à)
9 Ma mère veut … les magasins.	(faire, aller, acheter)
10 Mon frère Thomas est allé … Italie.	(en, sur, à)

Les verbes: conduire

The verb conduire is another of those slightly tricky verbs that it is worth learning by heart.

conduire	**to drive, to lead**
je conduis	nous conduisons
tu conduis	vous conduisez
il conduit	ils conduisent
participe passé: conduit	

Verbs that act like conduire:

produire	to produce
traduire	to translate
construire	to build, to construct

Negative questions

Changing sentences to make them questions, as well as negative

As you become better at French and use past and future expressions as well as present ones, it is important that you know how to change them to make questions and negatives. To do this, you simply have to:

- spot the auxiliary verb: this is the verb used to make compound tenses such as the perfect in il a mangé; the auxiliary is usually avoir but some verbs use être instead (il est parti), and aller is used for future tenses (il va partir).
- make all the changes to this auxiliary verb (avoir or être, or – in the case of the future – aller).

Let us try a few examples. First, remember how we make a passé composé expression negative, for example changing 'You looked' into 'You did not look':

Tu as regardé

In the negative, this becomes:

Tu n'as pas regardé

Now, we are going to make a question in the passé composé without using est-ce que:

Simply make a question by turning the subject and auxiliary verb around, putting a hyphen between the words. Thus, 'you have', 'he has', 'she has', become 'have you?', 'has he?', 'has she?':

Tu as regardé	As-tu regardé?

Note that with il a and elle a, -t- is inserted to make the phrase easy to pronounce. This is necessary when the verb before il or elle ends in a vowel:

Il a regardé	A-t-il regardé?
Elle a regardé	A-t-elle regardé?

Lastly, you just combine these rules to make a negative question ('haven't you ...?', 'didn't they ...?', and so on):

Tu as fini	N'as-tu pas fini?
Ils sont partis	Ne sont-ils pas partis?

The same goes for the futur proche, using aller + infinitive. You do all the changing to the aller part, then add the infinitive last:

Vous allez sortir Allez-vous sortir? N'allez-vous pas sortir?

To sum up

To say a passé composé or futur proche expression in the negative or as a question:

1 Make all the changes to the auxiliary verb (avoir, être or aller).
2 Add the past participle or infinitive.

Exercice 6.7

Rewrite these sentences in the passé composé, for example:

Je prends le déjeuner. **J'ai pris** le déjeuner.

1 Je conduis la voiture en Normandie.
2 Nous produisons de bons fromages.
3 Elle construit une maison en pierre.
4 Tu traduis le poème en anglais.
5 Marcel traduit l'affiche en français.

Pour aller plus loin ...

6 C'est toi qui conduis la voiture?
7 Non, je ne conduis jamais.
8 Qui construit ces maisons?
9 On produit le calvados en Normandie.

Exercice 6.8

Write these sentences as questions, for example:

Tu as fini. **As-tu** fini?

1 Ils ont terminé leur repas.
2 Elle a choisi une ferme-auberge.
3 Nous avons rempli le formulaire.
4 Tu as vendu la maison.
5 Vous avez vu l'hôtel.

Write these sentences in the negative, for example:

Elle a été **Elle n'a pas** été

6 Nous avons acheté le bracelet.
7 Il a aimé mon dessin.
8 Elles sont descendues.
9 Vous êtes restés.
10 Il est tombé.

Exercice 6.9

Listen to the audio.

Work in groups. Prepare and perform the dialogue.

La famille est arrivée à Pont-l'Evêque à midi, après un long trajet en voiture. Tout le monde est très content de pouvoir enfin descendre de la voiture. Maman a conduit vite sur l'autoroute, mais en ville elle a eu du mal à trouver l'office de tourisme. En arrivant, elle est fatiguée.

Maman. Ouf! Ces petites rues! On est où?

Tochiko. Rue Saint-Michel. Tiens! Voilà l'office de tourisme!

Maman. Tu crois qu'on a le droit de stationner ici?

Tochiko. Mais oui. Vas-y! [Tochiko descend de la voiture et entre dans l'office de tourisme.]

Employée. Bonjour!

Tochiko. Bonjour, madame. Puis-je avoir des informations sur la ville?

Employée. Mais bien sûr. Voici des dépliants. Il y a toutes sortes d'informations. Voulez vous autre chose?

Tochiko. Un plan de la ville, s'il vous plaît. C'est combien?

Employée.	C'est gratuit, mademoiselle.
Tochiko.	Merci, madame. Au revoir!
Employée.	Au revoir!

le trajet	journey
avoir le droit de (+ *inf.*)	to be allowed to, to have the right to
stationner	to park
vas-y!	go on!
le dépliant	leaflet
autre chose	something else
puis-je?	may I?

Exercice 6.10

Listen again to the audio for Exercice 6.9 and reread the introductory paragraph. Answer the questions in English.

1. What happened at midday?
2. What was everyone very happy to do?
3. How did Tochiko's mum drive?
4. How easy was it to find the tourist office?
5. How much did Tochiko have to pay for the map?

Exercice 6.11

Below is what happened next in the story, told by Tochiko.

Quand **je suis revenue** à la voiture, **j'ai vu** mon frère Pascal en train de téléphoner. **Maman a disparu**. **Marie-Christine a commencé** à se diriger vers l'église.

1. Take the four verb expressions and say what *did not* happen, for example if Tochiko said:

   Marie est arrivée à la gare.

   you would write:

   Marie n'est pas arrivée à la gare.

2. Copy the paragraph above and invent the next part of the story. Try to write five lines. If you are confident with the past tenses, then use them.

Exercice 6.12

Role play: At the tourist office

Take it in turns to be A and B. A starts the conversation.

A. Are there any restaurants?

B. Oui. Voici une liste.

A. Thank you. My friends are hungry!

B. Quelle sorte de cuisine aimez-vous?

A. [Answer the question.]

B. Alors, essayez Chez Toni, rue Lagarde.

A. Do I have to pay to park?

B. Non. De midi à 15 heures, c'est gratuit.

A. Tomorrow we are going to visit a farm.

B. Excellente idée.

A. Have you seen the weather forecast?

B. Oui, il va faire beau, mais pas chaud.

Exercice 6.13

Read the passage then do the exercise.

On discute dans la voiture, pour décider où manger. Il faut vite trouver un restaurant, parce qu'il est déjà midi et demi et la famille de Tochiko est nombreuse. Maman dit qu'elle est allée prendre une photo de l'église et qu'il y a une pizzeria dans une petite rue à côté. On décide d'y aller. Pascal et Mina adorent les pizzas, mais les autres choisissent des moules marinières. Maman mange des tagliatelles à la sauce forestière et elle boit de l'eau.

Après le repas, on remonte dans la voiture et on part à la recherche de la ferme-auberge. Elle s'appelle La Colombière. Elle se trouve à 6 km de Pont-l'Evêque et elle est «facile à voir de la route». Une demi-heure plus tard, maman tourne à droite et la famille se trouve sur une longue avenue bordée d'arbres, au bout de laquelle on voit enfin la ferme.

bordé de	lined with
au bout de laquelle	at the end of which
la sauce forestière	a creamy sauce with mushrooms

Match these questions to the answers that go with them:

1 Pourquoi y a-t-il une discussion dans la voiture?
2 Comment est-ce que maman a trouvé la pizzeria?
3 Qui aime les pizzas?
4 Le déjeuner fini, que fait la famille?
5 La Colombière, c'est quoi?

(a) Pascal et Mina les aiment.
(b) C'est une ferme-auberge.
(c) Elle part chercher la ferme-auberge.
(d) C'est pour décider où manger.
(e) Elle est allée prendre une photo de l'église; la pizzeria se trouve à côté.

Exercice 6.14

Tochiko talks about her holidays on the phone to Chloé. Choose the correct version of each phrase:

1 Salut! Comment es-tu?/Comment vas-tu?/Comment as-tu?
2 Nous avons enfin arrivé./Nous sommes enfin arrivés./Nous allons arriver.
3 Il fait froid/Il est froid/Il a froid
4 mais le soleil est brille/mais le soleil est brillant/mais le soleil brille
5 et je suis contente./et je suis content./et j'ai content.
6 Il y est des animaux/C'est des animaux/Il y a des animaux
7 partout./surtout./tout le monde.
8 Peux-tu ... téléphoner moi/me téléphoner/me téléphone
9 sur jeudi?/en jeudi?/jeudi?
10 Avoir!/Auvoir!/Au revoir!

Pour aller plus loin, traduis en français ...

11 I am well, thank you.
12 They (*f.*) arrived yesterday.
13 It is quite warm
14 ... but the sun is not shining now.
15 Can you phone me on Saturday?

Exercice 6.15

Texting definitely has its own language!

You have just arrived on holiday. It is raining but warm. You get this text from a friend ...

> Salu! j'SpR ke tu va bi1.
> qd étu AriV? kel temps
> fé til? Jé 1 Vlo 9, sé Gnial.
> @2m1, dak? biz, Marie

Try to answer it in the same way (if you understand it!). If not, your teacher will explain.

un texto	text message
neuf (*m.*), neuve (*f.*)	brand new
bises	love from (*lit.* kisses)

Exercice 6.16

106

Listen to the audio then answer the questions in English.

ça vaut la peine	it is worth the trouble
la boue	mud
la chèvre	goat
le mouton	sheep
au-delà de	beyond
le champ	field
une écurie	stable
la laiterie	dairy
appartenir	to belong
voisin (e)	neighbouring
la poule	hen
le poussin	chick
une oie	goose
la basse-cour	farmyard

1 What is the family's first impression of the ferme-auberge?

2 What does Marie-Christine ask Tochiko to do?

3 What is Tochiko's response?

4 Where are the sheep and goats?

5 What animals can they see in the farmyard?

Exercice 6.17

Around the class, pick out the verbs in this passage and say whether they are regular or irregular and, if they are regular, what group they belong to. Your teacher might ask you to take notes.

For example:

arrive	**présent**	**1er groupe**

La famille **arrive**. Tochiko descend, puis elle aide Marie-Christine. Marie-Christine a besoin de son fauteuil roulant, que maman sort de la voiture.

Pascal ne fait pas attention à la boue. Il court partout dans la basse-cour. Il voit beaucoup d'animaux. Mina compte douze animaux différents et elle écrit leurs noms dans son carnet. Marie-Christine est impatiente de dessiner. Elle veut commencer tout de suite, mais la famille va faire une promenade avant de prendre un bain et se changer pour le dîner.

Exercice 6.18

At the farm the internet is not very good. The family decide to read books and write the postcards they bought in the village.

You are Pascal or Mina. Write a postcard in French to your friend. Describe:

- arriving and finding the farm
- the weather
- the farmyard.

Don't forget Cher/Chère (...) at the beginning, and put Amitiés before signing off.

Exercice 6.19

1 Put the eight elements of this story in the right order. (a) is the first one.

(a) **Hier soir, on a mangé à la ferme.**

(b) Marie-Christine n'a pas aimé le sorbet.

(c) Maman a pris du café, mais pas les enfants.

(d) Le plat principal était du bœuf en croûte avec des carottes.

(e) Après l'assortiment de fromages normands, on a pu choisir un dessert du buffet.

(f) Comme entrée, on nous a proposé des asperges.

(g) Avant le fromage, on a mangé une salade.

(h) Pour nous préparer pour la viande, il y avait un sorbet à la pomme au calvados.

le sorbet	sorbet (often served before the main course)
en croûte	cooked in a pastry casing
normand	Norman (i.e. from Normandy)
on nous a proposé	we were offered
les asperges	asparagus
il y avait	there was/were
le calvados	Normandy apple brandy

Pour aller plus loin ...

2 Re-tell the story in English.

7 Novembre en Normandie

In this chapter you'll talk about activities and look at the imparfait – the imperfect tense – for the first time.

Exercice 7.1

Around the class, read the passage aloud. Read a little each. Translate the first, long, paragraph into English.

De retour à la maison, Tochiko et ses frères et sœurs se sont préparés pour retourner au collège. Ils se sont amusés en Normandie et ils ont maintenant de nouveaux amis, y compris des animaux! Ils ont appris beaucoup sur la vie à la campagne, qui est le contraire de la vie citadine. Ils ont pratiqué des activités qu'ils n'ont jamais eu la chance de pratiquer chez eux.

Magali et Chloé, elles, ont passé les vacances de la Toussaint chez elles, mais elles sont beaucoup sorties et elles sont parties visiter un vignoble du Val de Loire.

Bientôt, tous les jeunes se retrouvent à l'école.

Exercice 7.2

Listen to the audio. Answer the questions in English.

le bouchon	traffic jam (*originally* cork in a bottle)
embêter	to irritate
le déj	popular abbreviation of le déjeuner
ça tombe bien	that's worked out nicely
le calcul	arithmetic
de retour à la maison	on coming home

1 Which day did Tochiko and her family come home?

2 Why was there a traffic jam on the motorway?

3 What did maman not understand?

4 What lessons are the girls going to have before lunch?

5 Why does Chloé think that the English lesson will be difficult?

Exercice 7.3

Pascal is writing an email to his friend. There are nine mistakes. Write the correct version of each wrongly spelt word.

De: pascal@ ...

À: henri@ ...

Sujet: Salut

Je suis **rentrez** à la maison. Aujourd'hui, c'est lundi et on est en classe. On est **aller** en Normandie dans une ferme. Il y avait plein d'animaux. Mon animal **préférer**, c'est le cheval. Il a fait chaud mais il a **plus tout** les jours. Maman et Tochiko n'étaient pas **contente**. Il n'y avait pas de télé donc on a dû lire, écrire ou dessiner. On a **fais** des promenades et Marie-Christine **as** dessiné les oies et les **cochon**.

Réponds-moi vite

Pascal

Activités

A reminder of which verbs to use

Here are some verbs that we use with various activities. Note that jouer is used when playing a sport like tennis (jouer ***au*** tennis) and with musical instruments (jouer ***du*** piano). Faire is used where in English we use 'go' or 'do' (for example 'to go swimming', 'to do moto-cross'). However, aller is used in the phrase 'to go fishing': aller à la pêche.

- jouer + au, à la, à l', aux
- jouer + du, de la, de l', des (for a musical instrument)
- faire + du, de la, de l', des
- aller + au, à la, à l', aux

Exercice 7.4

Translate:

1 Chloé went climbing. — faire, escalade (*f.*)

2 The whole family went for walks in the forest. — tout, famille (*f.*), faire, promenade (*f.*), forêt (*f.*)

3 We played table tennis — jouer, ping-pong (*m.*)

4 Chloé's mother played chess with the owner. — mère (*f.*), jouer, échecs (*m.pl.*), propriétaire (*m./f.*)

5 Magali and Chloé played the guitar. — jouer, guitare (*f.*)

L'imparfait – The imperfect tense

The past tenses: a fuller explanation (2)

Here is a short passage with the verbs in *italics*. Look at the italics and try to say which verb each one comes from, for example:

je ***chantais*** comes from the verb ***chanter***

Can you see what endings are put on the verb? The answers are given at the end of this section.

Il ***faisait*** plus froid le matin et le soir, comme ça on ***savait*** que l'automne ***arrivait***. Les feuilles des arbres ***commençaient*** à changer de couleur. ***C'était*** un peu triste mais ***j'aimais*** cette saison parce que, quand ***j'étais*** petit, je ***m'amusais*** à jouer dans les feuilles mortes que mon père ***passait*** des heures à ramasser avec son râteau. Nous ***étions*** très contents!

ramasser	to gather up
râteau (*m.*)	rake

You will often see and hear expressions like:

c'était	it was
j'étais	I was

These are examples of the imparfait or *imperfect tense*.

The imparfait is best understood (in verbs other than être) as:

- was ...ing or were ...ing (e.g. I was playing, they were playing)
- used to ... (e.g. he used to buy a newspaper on Mondays).

The 'stem', or first part of the verb, is taken from the nous part of its present tense:

nous courons — we run (present)

- remove -ons
- add the correct ending: (il) cour + **ait** (the right ending for il)

So that the expression 'he was running' would be il courait.

This makes the imparfait an easy tense to understand and to use.

There is only one exception:

The stem for être is ét-, which you have seen before, in c'était and j'étais.

Did you get them right?

Here are the answers:

il **faisait** plus froid	faire	it (the weather) was colder
on **savait**	savoir	one/we knew
l'automne **arrivait**	arriver	autumn was arriving/autumn was on its way
les feuilles des arbres **commençaient**	commencer	the leaves on the trees began/were beginning
c'**était**	être	it was
j'**aimais**	aimer	I liked/I used to like
j'**étais**	être	I was/I used to be
je m'**amusais**	s'amuser	I had fun/I used to have fun
mon père **passait**	passer	my father spent/used to spend (time)
nous **étions**	être	we were

So the endings are:

je tu il elle	-ais -ais -ait -ait	nous vous ils elles	-ions -iez -aient aient
on	-ait		

... and **all** verbs in French have the same endings in the imparfait!

Exercice 7.5

A little practice with the imparfait: write these sentences with the verbs in the imperfect tense, as in the example:

Mon copain jouait du piano.

1 Maman (jouer) au tennis.

2 Le père de Magali (faire) de l'équitation.

3 Mon frère (jouer) au golf.

4 Quand il était jeune, il (faire) de la planche à voile.

5 Magali et Pauline (faire) de la voile.

Exercice 7.6

Translate:

1 The lady was singing in the kitchen.	dame (*f.*), chanter, cuisine (*f.*)
2 A man was reading the newspaper.	homme (*m.*), lire, journal (*m.*)
3 Their house was old and interesting.	maison (*f.*), être, vieux (*f.* vieille), intéressant
4 My brother was playing guitar.	frère (*m.*), jouer (de + musical instrument), guitare (*f.*)
5 Sabine's mum used to watch television on Sundays.	mère (*f.*), regarder, télévision (*f.*), dimanche

Reminder: Have you checked that your adjectives **agree** with the nouns they describe?

Exercice 7.7

Listen to the audio and note the vocabulary.

la côte de porc	pork chop
fade	tasteless
la découverte	discovery
le terrain	ground, games pitch
le stade	stadium
bien s'entendre (avec quelqu'un)	to get on (with someone)
la randonnée	hike, hiking

Answer the questions in English:

1. What did Tochiko think of her pork chop?
2. How do we know the girls are fed up with hearing how good the food was on Tochiko's holiday?
3. What does Tochiko say to further tease them?
4. Where was Pascal playing football?
5. What did Pascal say about Normandy?
6. How did he get on with the brothers he met there?
7. What outdoor activities did they all do, apart from using mountain bikes?

Exercice 7.8

Complete the sentences by selecting the right word for each gap.

1 Tochiko pensait que son déjeuner était …	(délicieux/intéressant/fade)
2 La cuisine à la ferme était …	(normale/intéressante/délicieuse)
3 La cuisinière a préparé des plats …	(différents/dégoûtants/drôles)
4 Tochiko … où Magali se trouve.	(ne suit pas/ne sait pas/ne peut pas)
5 Pascal … bien avec les frères.	(s'entend/s'attend/s'étend)

Exercice 7.9

Match these phrases to their French translations:

1 **it was horrible**	(a) je l'ai vue ce matin
2 what did you have?	(b) de nouveaux amis
3 not like the cooking at the farm	(c) pas comme la cuisine à la ferme
4 right, OK	(d) bon, d'accord
5 that's enough!	(e) **c'était dégoûtant**
6 why don't we talk about something else?	(f) ça suffit!
7 I don't know about Magali	(g) Magali, je ne sais pas
8 I saw her this morning	(h) si on parlait d'autre chose?
9 some new friends	(i) des tas de choses
10 lots of things	(j) tu as pris quoi?

Exercice 7.10

Translate, not forgetting to look for clues in the previous exercises.

1 it was delicious
2 what did you drink?
3 not like the walks at the beach
4 why don't we play tennis?
5 why don't we phone Christine?
6 why don't you (*sing.*) buy that T-shirt?
7 I don't know about you (*pl.*)

8 we saw it (*m.*) yesterday evening

9 some old buildings

10 some big cars

Pour aller plus loin ...

11 it wasn't difficult

12 what did you (*pl.*) see?

13 why don't we go home?

14 some important people

Exercice 7.11

Complete this email message by filling in the gaps with words from the box below.

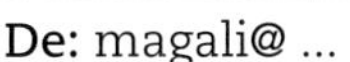

De: magali@ ...

À: tochiko@ ...

Objet: Le livre sur La Roche

Salut Peter

Merci pour ton e-mail. Je l'ai reçu mardi matin. Tu m'as demandé de t'envoyer le beau livre sur La Roche. Je l'ai vu ce ... quand je suis ... en ville. Maman a ... ton stylo aussi. Elle l'a trouvé ... la table. Elle t'a envoyé un ... ce matin.

À bientôt!

Amicalement,

Magali

colis	cherché	sous	envoyé
matin	reçu	allée	

Exercice 7.12

Which titles go with which information? Choose the correct titles from the options below to match the numbers with the letters.

1 Ouvert toute l'année sauf le 25 décembre et Pâques. Service les midi et soir du mardi au samedi 12h–15h et 19h–21h.

2 Formule Mousquetaire: entrée, plat et dessert 16€.

Formule Chevalier: plat et dessert ou entrée et plat 11€.

3 Stationnement limité à 30 minutes, interdit le 1er et 3e mardi du mois.

4 Mercredi 20 heures *Spectre* version originale avec sous-titres français (VOST).

5 Petit, très mignon, âgé de 8 mois, de race persane, on ne l'a pas vu depuis le 14 juillet dans la soirée. Récompense.

Titles:

(a) Chat perdu

(b) Parking, Place du Marché

(c) Menu

(d) Cette semaine au Dragon

(e) Horaires d'ouverture

Exercice 7.13

Prepared talk: A regional or national celebration

Prepare to talk for 30 seconds on this topic. Be ready to say:

- where you came across this celebration (e.g. somewhere you went on holiday)
- when it took place (e.g. 14 July – le 14 juillet)
- what it celebrates (e.g. the storming of the Bastille prison in Paris in 1789).

This is about the length you need to speak for (this one is 51 words):

Je vais parler de la Fête nationale du quatorze juillet. J'étais en vacances. On visitait Poitiers avec mes parents. Le quatorze juillet, c'est pour fêter la prise de la Bastille en 1789. Il y avait un défilé militaire dans la rue. C'était magnifique. Le soir, il y avait un feu d'artifice.

Then you need to respond to a few questions about what you have just said.

Exercice 7.14

Write one short sentence for each image, in the present, past and future (aller + infinitive) tenses, for example:

Au présent:	**Aujourd'hui** ma sœur **fait** du cheval.
Au passé:	**Vendredi dernier**, ma sœur **a fait** du cheval.
Au futur:	**Samedi prochain***, ma sœur **va faire** du cheval.
* prochain	next

1

2

3

4

5

Exercice 7.15

You have arrived in Paris on holiday. Write an email of 80–120 words in French to a friend. You must mention **four** of the following points. Don't forget to use past, present and future verb tenses, and show a good range of vocabulary and grammar.

- the journey — le voyage
- the hotel — l'hôtel
- the meals — les repas
- a new friend — un nouvel ami/une nouvelle amie
- a problem — un problème

Exercice 7.16

Le centre sportif

Pendant les vacances, Magali et Chloé sont beaucoup sorties. Avec leurs parents, elles sont allées au théâtre, à un concert de musique classique et dans un centre sportif énorme à Nantes. Voici l'affiche que les filles ont vue en entrant dans le centre sportif.

Centre Sportif de Sainte-Madeleine

Grande salle – sports collectifs (volley, handball, basket, etc.)

5 courts de squash (sur réservation)

Piscine surveillée en permanence

Garderie (sauf le week-end)

Horaire d'ouverture

Tous les jours ouvrables sauf le jeudi, de 8 h 30 à 12 h 15 et de 14 h à 20 h

Le jeudi et le samedi de 9 h à 20 h sans interruption.

Le dimanche et les jours fériés: fermé

Entrée

Adultes 5 € 50

Juniors (de 12 à 17 ans) 3 € 50

Enfants (moins de 12 ans) 1 € 50

Parking

Durée	Prix
0 à 2h	gratuit
2h + 0, 50 €/h	
Cars scolaires	nous consulter

Cafétéria (ouvert de 12 à 14 h et de 15 h à 19 h)

La cafétéria est située au premier étage du bâtiment.

Pour votre sécurité, le parking est sous vidéo-surveillance 24h/24h

le sport collectif	team sport
surveiller	to watch over
la garderie/crèche	crèche
sauf	except
un horaire	timetable
le jour ouvrable	weekday
le jour férié	holiday
le groupe scolaire	a school party
quitter	to leave

Say whether the following statements are true or false (vrai ou faux).

1 I am 15, so I can go in the sports centre for 3 € 50.

2 My sister, who is 12, must pay the same as me.

3 My father, mother, sister and I can all get in for less than 20 €.

4 You can leave the car in the car park for 2 hours without paying.

5 There is no lifeguard in the pool during the evenings.

Exercice 7.17

Translate:

1 There are sometimes school groups at the sports centre.	quelquefois, groupe (*m.*) scolaire
2 I can't go to the sports centre on Sunday.	pouvoir, aller, dimanche (*m.*)
3 On Thursdays, the swimming pool is closed at lunchtime.	jeudi, piscine (*f.*), fermé, midi
4 You can eat without leaving the sports centre.	pouvoir, sans (+ *infin.*), quitter
5 There are three sports centres in Nantes.	centre sportif (*m.*)

Exercice 7.18

Des excuses, des excuses!

Look at this example. It is a voicemail message. Who is phoning? What is the message about?

Allô? C'est **Armand**! Je suis désolé, je suis **à la maison**, il est **midi**. Je ne peux pas venir, j'ai **cassé mes lunettes**!

Allô? C'est Armand!

Here are some situations. Work in pairs. Phone your partner to say why you are late. Leave a message on their voicemail – they must jot down the details. Then swap roles.

Qui tu es	Où tu es	L'heure	Pourquoi tu es en retard: tu as ...	
Paul	**à la maison**	10 h 30	raté	tes cahiers
Sophie	à Nantes	14 h	perdu	tes clés
Armand	à l'aéroport	9 h	oublié	**tes lunettes**
Georges	à Londres	minuit	**cassé**	une longue promenade
Philippe	au stade	**midi**	mangé	le chat
Pierre	à la gare	17 h	fait	l'avion
Marie				le bus
Létitia				ton vélo
Jean-Luc				tes livres
Patrick				tes livres
Sabine				trop de pizza
Stéphane				trop de bananes

la messagerie	voicemail
rater	to miss, to fail (an exam)

Hier, aujourd'hui et demain

In this chapter you'll learn something about television in France and the uses of the verb se mettre.

Exercice 8.1

109

Read the passage and listen to the audio. Study the vocabulary.

Magali, Chloé, Tochiko, Marie-Christine et Pascal sont au café près du collège, le Café des Amis. Ils parlent de leur journée d'école et de leur temps libre. Ils parlent de ce qu'ils ont fait, et de ce qu'ils vont faire. Heureusement, l'accès pour les handicapés est facile. Les jeunes gens doivent se mettre à l'intérieur du café car il va pleuvoir et il fait déjà un peu froid. Le café est bondé. Le serveur arrive.

bondé(e)	crowded
vous êtes prêts à ...	are you ready to ...?
une rédaction	essay
mettre deux heures à ...	to take two hours to ...
le documentaire	documentary
le docu	(abbreviation) documentary
genre James Bond	a James Bond type of thing
des sous-titres (*m.pl.*)	subtitles
s'amuser	to have a good time, to enjoy oneself
rigolo	funny
étranger	foreign
il me reste (une heure)	I have (one hour) left

Answer the questions in English. Answers to questions 1 and 2 are in the printed passage above, but the rest are on the audio.

1 Why do the young people need to get inside the café?

2 What do they talk about?

3 What does the waiter ask them first?

4 What does Pascal have to drink?

5 When is Tochiko going to do her homework?

6 What is on France 2 this evening?

7 Where was Magali expected to be the previous evening?

8 Where was she in fact?

Exercice 8.2

Say which questions go with which answers.

1 Qu'est-ce que tu prends?

2 Qu'est-ce que tu as fait?

3 Ça dure combien de temps?

4 C'était comment?

5 Tu as quoi comme devoirs?

(a) C'était super, très amusant.

(b) Je suis allée au cinéma.

(c) Pour moi, un coca, s'il te plaît.

(d) J'ai de l'espagnol et des maths.

(e) Normalement, une heure.

La télévision en France – Television in France

La télévision en France est comme partout ailleurs: une vingtaine de chaînes gratuites et un choix étonnant de chaînes par satellite et câble. En France il y a beaucoup de chaînes qu'on peut recevoir sans payer d'abonnement et des chaînes cryptées qui nécessitent un décodeur pour être reçues en clair.

Les chaînes principales sont:

- TF1
- France 2
- France 3
- France 5
- M6
- Arte

La chaîne cryptée la plus connue s'appelle Canal Plus (Canal+).

comme partout ailleurs	like everywhere else
la chaîne	channel
étonnant	astonishing
un abonnement	subscription
crypté	encrypted
le décodeur	decoder
en clair	decrypted, decoded, clear
le programme	schedule for radio or TV programmes
une émission	an individual programme

Voici quelques genres d'émission:

une émission sportive	a sport programme
un feuilleton	a soap
un documentaire	a documentary
un polar	a police detective film
les infos/les informations/le journal télévisé	the news
la météo	the weather forecast

Exercice 8.3

Here is part of the television schedule for an evening in November:

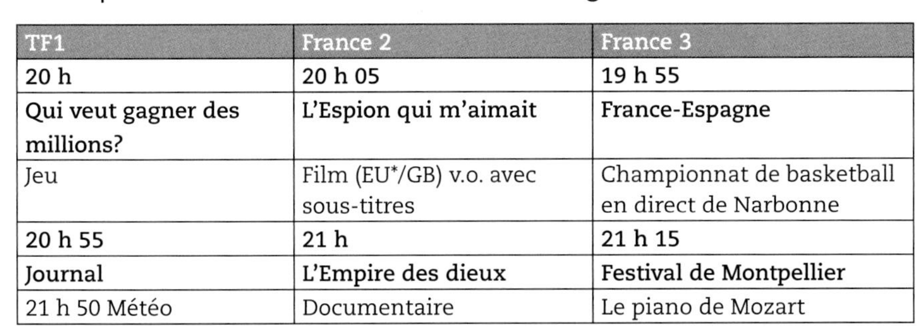

TF1	France 2	France 3
20 h	**20 h 05**	**19 h 55**
Qui veut gagner des millions?	**L'Espion qui m'aimait**	**France-Espagne**
Jeu	Film (EU*/GB) v.o. avec sous-titres	Championnat de basketball en direct de Narbonne
20 h 55	**21 h**	**21 h 15**
Journal	**L'Empire des dieux**	**Festival de Montpellier**
21 h 50 Météo	Documentaire	Le piano de Mozart

* EU **Not** the European Union, but les États-Unis (USA)

Decide which programmes would appeal to these people:

Jean aime le football, mais pas d'autres sports. Il s'intéresse au cinéma américain et il adore la musique.

Claudine va faire de la voile demain s'il fait beau. Elle aime essayer de répondre aux questions de culture générale.

Justine s'intéresse beaucoup à l'histoire des civilisations anciennes. Elle est aussi très sportive.

Jonathan aime se détendre en regardant un film qui n'est pas trop sérieux. Il aime aussi savoir ce qui se passe dans le monde.

Marc aime les langues: il écoute souvent la radio anglaise. Il fait partie de l'orchestre du collège.

v.o., VO	version originale (not dubbed)
ce qui se passe	what is happening
le monde	the world
la culture	knowledge

Exercice 8.4

Role play

You are at a French friend's house. You (A) talk with your friend (B) about what to watch on TV. Take it in turns to be A and B. B begins.

B. Qu'est-ce que tu veux regarder à la télé?

A. I don't know – what is there?

B. Du sport, un docu, un polar?

A. I like cycling or football.

B. Il y a le Tour, mais il n'y a pas de foot ce soir.

A. May I watch the Tour?

B. Oui, bien sûr. Tu fais du cyclisme, toi?

A. Yes, every Sunday.

B. Moi non, mais j'aime regarder le Tour.

A. Why do you like it?

B. J'aime voir les paysages, la campagne.

A. Yes, it's really interesting.

Exercice 8.5

How good are your verbs? This exercise will help you to find out. Copy the passage with the correct French for the verbs in brackets. Use the passé composé (action) or imparfait (description) for each verb, as necessary.

Quand Chloé (went out), elle (saw) Magali, qui (was walking) le chien de sa copine. Elle (asked) à Magali si maman (was) en ville. Magali (answered) qu'elle ne (know) pas, mais elle (said) qu'elle (thought) que maman (was ordering) du pain pour dimanche.

to go out sortir
to walk (e.g. a dog) promener
to ask demander
to answer répondre
to know savoir
to say dire
to order commander
en ville in town

Les verbes: se mettre

The verb se mettre means 'to put oneself', which is an expression we don't often use in English! As you may have noticed, it can be an alternative in French for 'to sit' or 'to stand' somewhere.

Note also that se mettre **à** + infinitive means 'to begin to', for example:

je me suis mis à travailler I began to work

se mettre	to put oneself*
je me mets	nous nous mettons
tu te mets	vous vous mettez
il se met	ils se mettent
elle se met	elles se mettent
participe passé: mis	

* This is simply the reflexive version of the irregular verb mettre – to put.

Here are some reminders of how it looks in other tenses:

Au passé composé: je me suis mis(e)
À l'imparfait: je me mettais
Au futur proche: je vais me mettre

Exercice 8.6

Une journée de voile à Bretignolles-sur-Mer

Before you read the story, look through the vocabulary. Read the passage, then do the exercise.

une station balnéaire a seaside resort
le mal de mer sea-sickness
le permis licence
le gilet de sauvetage life-jacket
même even, same
paraître to appear, to seem
nautique nautical
le dériveur dinghy

la fusée éclairante	flare
le moniteur	the instructor
la caution	deposit

Une promenade en mer

1 C'était vendredi. Papa a promis à Chloé et Magali de les emmener le lendemain faire de la voile à Bretignolles, une station balnéaire. À Bretignolles, sur la côte vendéenne, c'était possible de louer des bateaux.

2 Samedi donc, papa, Magali et Chloé ont quitté la maison après un petit-déjeuner rapide. En route, ils ont acheté du pain, du fromage, des tomates, des poires et de l'eau pour faire un pique-nique à midi.

3 Chloé a lu le prospectus du club. Elle a découvert qu'il fallait avoir un permis bateau. C'était même interdit pour les mineurs (les jeunes de moins de dix-huit ans) de partir sans un adulte à bord. De plus, on était obligé de mettre des gilets de sauvetage et d'apporter des fusées éclairantes. Elle a demandé à papa si tout cela était vraiment nécessaire. Il a répondu que la mer était dangereuse, même si elle paraissait calme.

4 En arrivant au club nautique, papa et les deux jeunes filles sont descendus de la voiture et sont allés chercher un dériveur à louer. Il faisait un temps parfait. La mer était calme et le soleil brillait. Pourtant, on pouvait voir un nuage noir à l'horizon.

5 Le moniteur du club est venu et papa a loué un petit bateau à quatre places. On lui a demandé une caution de 300 euros! Tout le monde est entré dans l'eau et papa a ordonné aux enfants de pousser le bateau.

Match these headings to the numbered paragraphs above. One is not required.

(a) La promesse

(b) On fait le tour de Bretignolles

(c) On prépare un pique-nique

(d) C'est papa qui paie!

(e) La météo

(f) Il faut respecter la mer

Exercice 8.7

Reread the story in Exercice 8.6 and answer the questions in English.

1 What had papa promised to do?
2 Where is Bretignolles?
3 What did Chloé do on the journey?
4 What do you need a licence for?
5 What age must you be to go sailing on your own?

Exercice 8.8

Here are some items typically used to prepare a picnic. Look up any you don't know and write down their meanings.

du pain
du saucisson
des chips
des oranges
des yaourts
des salades préparées
du vin

du beurre
du jambon
de la confiture
des pommes
du chocolat
du thon
de l'eau

de l'Orangina
du fromage
du poulet
des poires
des bananes
des carottes râpées
du coca

Exercice 8.9

Work in pairs.

Make a list in French of **five** things from the list in Exercice 8.8 that *you* would take on a picnic. Do not show each other. Then get your partner to guess what you have written. In French only, of course.

Exercice 8.10

Prepared talk: A sports personality

Prepare to talk for 30 seconds on a sports personality of your choice. Be ready to:

- explain his or her connection with France
- say why you like him or her
- speak a little about the last time you saw him or her in action.

For example:

Je vais parler de Charline Picon. Elle est championne française de voile et elle a gagné une médaille d'or à Rio aux Jeux olympiques. Je ne suis pas allé(e) à Rio, mais je l'ai vue à la télé. Elle était championne d'Europe de voile en 2013, 2014 et 2016.

You need to be ready to answer a few questions about your subject, so research it online in good time. Use the French versions of general information websites.

Some possible questions might be along these lines:

- Elle a quel âge, Charline Picon?
- Comment s'appelle le champion de voile anglais/la championne de voile anglaise?
- Tu fais aussi de la voile?
- Dans ton école, on peut faire de la voile?
- Pourquoi est-ce que tu aimes la voile?

Exercice 8.11

Read as you listen to the audio. Prepare and present the dialogue in class.

Sur la plage, après la promenade en bateau.

Chloé.	Merci, papa, c'était épatant!
Papa.	Attendez là, je reviens!
Chloé.	J'ai froid.
Magali.	Si tu avais ton pull ...
Chloé.	Je vais l'apporter la prochaine fois.
Magali.	La mer était belle. Elle était assez calme.
Chloé.	Oui. Je n'aime pas quand elle est agitée.
Magali.	Tu avais peur.
Chloé.	Mais non ...
Papa.	Tenez, je viens d'acheter des gaufres.
Magali.	Mmm! J'adore ça!
Papa.	Tu veux la grande ou la petite?
Magali.	La grande, s'il te plaît, papa.
Papa.	Alors, l'autre est pour moi!
Chloé.	Et moi?
Papa.	Oh! Tu veux une gaufre aussi? Tiens ...
Chloé.	Merci, papa chéri!

je reviens	I'll be back	agité	rough
épatant	amazing	une gaufre	waffle

Exercice 8.12

The verbs are highlighted in this passage. Give their infinitives. Some are already infinitives, of course.

Mina **voulait** aller au concert de Danny Lefou à La Roche, mais elle **n'a pas acheté** de billets parce qu'elle **n'a pas vu** les annonces dans le journal. Toutes les filles de la classe de Mina **sont** folles de Danny Lefou. Il **joue** de la guitare et il **chante** avec son groupe de quatre autres musiciens de rock qui **font** un bruit inimaginable. Il **vient** rarement dans l'ouest de la France.

Mina **a** de la chance, parce que sa sœur Tochiko **a remarqué** la publicité pour le concert et **a acheté** trois billets. Comme ça, Mina **a pu** emmener une amie avec elle. Le concert **a été** un grand succès. Pendant l'entracte, Mina **a acheté** un T-shirt et un CD signés par son idole. Quand Mina et Natalie **sont revenues** à la maison, elles **étaient** très animées et elles **n'arrêtaient pas** d'en parler.

Le lendemain, Natalie **a aidé** Mina à nettoyer le garage!

Exercice 8.13

Design a poster for French people living in England, for one appearance by a French musician or group who are doing a tour in the UK.

The group (make up a name!) will perform:

- on **Saturday 13 July**
- at the **Maison Française in Oxford**
- at **half-past seven** in the evening

Admission is **£8**:

- but **under-14s pay half price**
- you can buy **T-shirts and CDs** after the concert

Exercice 8.14

Role play: Au concert

You (A) go to an open-air concert with a friend (B). Take it in turns to be A and B.

A. Do you have the tickets?

B. Il n'y a pas de billets.

A. Why?

B. C'est gratuit!

A. That's great. Where can we sit?

B. Où on veut …

Si on se mettait … là?

A. That's fine!

B. Il y a des concerts en plein air en Angleterre?

A. Yes, if it doesn't rain!

B. Tu aimes quoi, comme musique, toi?

A. [Answer the question.]

9 Le séjour de Peter en France

In this chapter you'll follow Peter's stay in France and remind yourself about adverbs.

Exercice 9.1

111

Read the passage and listen to the audio, then answer the questions.

Peter, le correspondant anglais de Chloé, est arrivé le 12 décembre. Il était seulement dix-sept heures, mais il faisait déjà noir. Après une journée de pluie et de vent, il faisait froid: l'hiver arrivait.

Ni Chloé ni Magali n'ont dû aller à l'école cet après-midi, car c'était un mercredi. Donc, à seize heures trente, maman et les filles sont allées chercher Peter à l'aéroport.

ni ... ni ... ne (+ *verb*)	neither ... nor

1 Peter est arrivé dans ... (la matinée/l'après-midi/la soirée)

2 Il faisait un temps ... (estival/agréable/froid)

3 Quand il est arrivé, il ... (faisait noir/faisait jour/neigeait)

Exercice 9.2

112

Listen to the audio and answer the questions in English.

reconnaître	to recognise
avoir le droit de (+ *infin.*)	to be allowed to
un crème	a milky coffee
la douane	the customs

1 Why could the family not meet Peter straight away?

2 What did maman suggest they do while waiting?

3 On what condition did Chloé agree?

4 Why do you think Chloé had tea *with milk*?

5 How did Peter seem when they met him?

6 What did Peter like about the journey?

Exercice 9.3

Choose a word from the box below for each gap. One has been done for you.

C'est toujours … de voyager en avion, parce qu'… trop de monde aux aéroports. L'année **dernière**, ma tante canadienne est … en Europe avec Doug et Charles, mes …. Pour … l'Atlantique, ils ont … un voyage de treize heures. Leur voyage a commencé à quatre heures du …! Ils ont passé leur temps à … dans les files d'attente, passer à l'enregistrement, faire contrôler leurs bagages et ce n'est qu'à dix … qu'ils sont finalement … par la passerelle dans l'avion pour Paris.

cousins	fatigant	attendre	heures	il y a
monté	**dernière**	traverser	venue	fait
matin	amusant	traversé	montés	cousines

Exercice 9.4

You are at the airport. There is free wi-fi. Write an email in French to a friend, in 80 to 120 words. You must mention at least **four** of these five points:

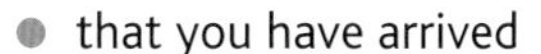

- that you have arrived — que tu es arrivé(e)
- what the flight was like — le vol
- what the weather is like — le temps qu'il fait
- why you will be late — pourquoi tu vas être en retard
- what you have done to pass the time — ce que tu as fait pour te divertir

Exercice 9.5

Say which questions would go with which answers.

1 Où sont les toilettes, s'il vous plaît?

2 Pour aller à la gare?

3 On peut acheter une boisson chaude ici?

4 Où peut-on acheter un journal?

5 Les départs, c'est ici au rez-de-chaussée?

(a) Non, il faut monter à l'étage.

(b) La maison de la presse est à gauche.

(c) Elles sont au fond, derrière le café.

(d) Oui, le Café Rouge est toujours ouvert.

(e) Continuez tout droit, c'est tout près.

Exercice 9.6

Match the sentence halves then copy them in full to make eight correct sentences.

1 Les aéroports sont fatigants	(a) je téléphone à mes parents.
2 Le parking	(b) a joué sur sa PlayStation®.
3 On n'a pas le droit de laisser	(c) mais ils sont nécessaires.
4 Le vol Paris-Rome était assez court	(d) que j'ai lu après le dîner.
5 Quand j'arrive en France,	(e) les bagages sans surveillance.
6 Dans le taxi en route pour l'hôtel, mon frère	(f) et très confortable.
7 J'ai acheté un magazine	(g) de trouver les toilettes pour handicapés.
8 C'était difficile	(h) est à côté du restaurant Les Alizés.

En

An important word with many uses

As you know, en can mean 'of it', 'of them', 'some' or 'any'.

He has **some**.	Il **en** a.
Does he have **any**?	**En** a-t-il?
He has three **of them**.	Il **en** a trois.
He has a litre **of it**.	Il **en** a un litre.

When doing the next exercise, remember that we can leave out 'of it', 'of them', and so on, in English **but not in French**:

You bought three the other day.	Tu **en** as acheté trois l'autre jour.

... because 'you bought three' really means 'you bought three **of them**'.

Exercice 9.7

Traduis en français:

1 Jean-Paul has thirty of them.
2 The cat is eating one of them.
3 We are looking at some.
4 I ate seven of them last week.
5 Do you want any?
6 They have some in the kitchen.
7 There is a litre of it in the fridge.
8 Why don't you have some?
9 Philippe has twelve of them.
10 I do not have any.

Pour aller plus loin …

11 She has twenty.

12 There are six.

13 We have two in the garage.

14 They are watching one (*m.*).

15 I read one yesterday.

Exercice 9.8

The titles for these paragraphs are **wrong**! Put them with the right paragraphs by writing a number, followed by the right title:

La salle de bains

1 Peter s'est installé chez les Colbert. Il parlait bien français pour un Anglais de son âge, mais il avait oublié beaucoup de vocabulaire, donc Chloé lui a fait visiter la maison, en lui rappelant tous les mots français pour les meubles, les objets et le décor.

Peter va dormir ici

2 D'abord, ils sont entrés dans la cuisine, où Chloé lui a montré les couverts sur la table, c'est-à-dire la nappe, les couteaux, les fourchettes, les cuillères, les assiettes et les verres. Elle lui a montré les placards et les appareils électroménagers: le lave-linge, le lave-vaisselle, le frigo, le congélateur et la cafetière électrique. Elle lui a indiqué les casseroles, le four à micro-ondes et la cuisinière à gaz. Il n'y avait pas de moquette au rez-de-chaussée, il y avait du carrelage.

On fait le tour de la maison

3 Magali a fermé les volets et les fenêtres et tiré les rideaux. Les trois jeunes gens sont montés à l'étage, où se trouvaient les chambres. Il y en a quatre: la chambre des parents, celles de Chloé et de Magali et la chambre des invités, provisoirement la chambre de Peter.

Ici, on prépare les repas

4 Dans la chambre de Peter il y avait un lit avec deux oreillers et une couette, une commode, une armoire, une petite table, une chaise, une lampe et un réveil sur la table de chevet. Il y avait aussi une petite étagère avec quelques livres.

Le soir chez les Colbert

5 Dans la petite pièce à l'étage, il y avait une douche, un lavabo, des serviettes et les brosses à dents de toute la famille, un tapis par terre et une glace au mur. A côté du radiateur, il y avait une petite poubelle. La fenêtre de la salle de bains donnait sur la cour derrière la maison.

elle lui a montré	she showed him (literally *to* him)
les meubles	the furniture
le décor	the decor
le placard	cupboard

les appareils électroménagers (*m.pl.*)	household appliance(s)
le lave-linge	washing machine
le lave-vaisselle	dishwasher
la cafetière électrique	electric coffee machine
la casserole	saucepan
la cuisinière à gaz	gas cooker
le four à micro-ondes	microwave
la moquette	fitted carpet
le carrelage	tiling
le frigo	fridge
le congélateur	freezer
les rideaux	curtains
tirer les rideaux	to draw the curtains
provisoirement	temporarily
un oreiller	pillow
la couette	duvet
le réveil	alarm clock
l'étagère (*f.*)	shelf
la douche	shower
le tapis	rug
la glace	mirror
donner sur	to look out onto
la cour	courtyard

Exercice 9.9

Reread the paragraphs from Exercice 9.8 and answer the questions in English.

1. Why did Chloé and Magali take Peter round the house?
2. Which room did they go into first?
3. What sort of floor did it have?
4. Did the Colberts have a bath tub or a shower?
5. Which room had become Peter's, temporarily?

Exercice 9.10

Work in pairs. Ask each other these questions. Write down the answers, then check your notes with your partner.

1 À quelle heure t'es-tu couché(e) hier soir?

2 À quelle heure te lèves-tu le dimanche matin?

3 Tu vas à l'école le samedi?

4 Qu'est-ce que tu fais après les classes?

5 Comment (par quel moyen de transport) est-ce que tu vas à l'école?

Exercice 9.11

Peter's bike ride

Read the passage and use it to help you complete the exercise that follows it.

1 A dix heures du matin, après avoir pris le petit-déjeuner avec Madame Colbert, Peter a emprunté la bicyclette de Magali et a fait un tour dans les environs de la maison. Avant de se mettre en route, il a examiné le vélo et il s'est demandé s'il connaissait tous les noms français des différentes parties du vélo.

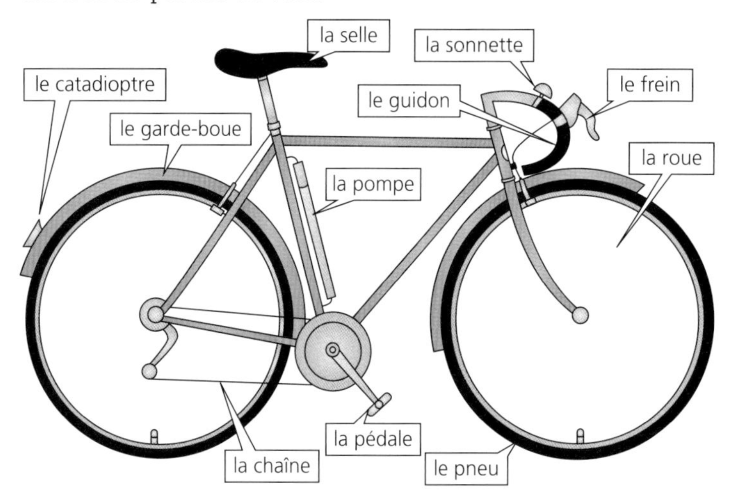

2 Puis il est parti. Il n'avait fait que deux cents mètres quand il s'est arrêté tout d'un coup.

«Que je suis idiot!» s'est-il dit. «Je roule à gauche, comme en Angleterre! Ici on roule à droite! C'est dangereux!» Il a traversé la route avec prudence, puis il est remonté sur la bicyclette et s'est remis en route. Il est passé devant l'église et a redécouvert tous les magasins du village.

3 Au lieu de traverser la place, Peter est descendu de la bicyclette et a fait le tour du camping municipal du village à pied. Il a regardé les annonces affichées au mur de la réception du camping. Il en a compris quelques-unes, mais pas toutes.

4 Il faisait froid, mais beau. Malgré le froid, on sentait le soleil. Il y avait une rosée légère dans les champs et Peter pensait à Chloé et Magali qui étaient à l'école. Chloé, souriante, sociable, positive et Magali, têtue et impulsive mais gentille et sincère.

5 Peter roulait lentement pour rentrer à la maison. Il était content d'être de nouveau en France.

Maman. Salut, Peter! Alors, ça a été?

Peter. Oui, madame. La campagne est belle.

Maman. J'ai une surprise pour toi. Samedi, on va partir en vacances de neige!

Peter. Formidable! Où va-t-on aller?

Maman. La station s'appelle Les Gêts. On va louer un chalet!

Peter. Chouette!

Maman. Tu as déjà fait du ski?

Peter. Non, jamais. Où se trouvent Les Gêts?

Maman. Regarde. J'ai une carte ici sur la table.

ça a été?	was it good?
les environs	the surrounding area
se mettre en route	to set off
rouler	to go along (in or on a wheeled vehicle)
avec prudence	with care
au lieu de	instead of
municipal	belonging to the local council
une annonce	advertisement
afficher	to post (i.e. to pin up on a notice board)
quelques-un(e)s	some
la rosée	dew
têtu	headstrong, stubborn
impulsif	impulsive
sincère	sincere
de nouveau	once again

Give a title to each of the numbered paragraphs. Choose from these options. One of them is not needed.

(a) Le retour
(b) Une pause à pied
(c) Pas comme chez nous!
(d) Les amies de Peter
(e) Le clocher de l'église
(f) Un tour à vélo

Exercice 9.12

Imagine you are Peter. Write an email to a friend of 80–120 words in French, in which you talk about your first day back at the Colberts' house. You must mention **four** of the following five points:

- your arrival — ton arrivée
- the bike ride — le tour à vélo
- the village and its campsite — le village et son camping
- the weather — le temps qu'il fait
- Madame Colbert's surprise news — la surprise de Mme Colbert

Exercice 9.13

Role play: On réserve un chalet

You (A) phone an agency (B) to ask if it is possible to book a ski chalet. B starts.

B. Bonjour, Agence Ski-famille?

A. Hello, I'd like to book a chalet in Les Gêts.

B. Oui, j'ai deux chalets disponibles. C'est pour quand?

A. It's for next week, from the 14th.

B. Et vous êtes combien?

A. We are five: three children and two adults.

B. C'est possible, mais il y a une autre famille.

A. That's fine.

B. C'est à quel nom, s'il vous plaît?

A. [Answer the question.]

B. Et ça s'écrit comment?

A. [Spell out your surname (in French!).]

Exercice 9.14

Translate:

1 I am going to buy a lovely book in my aunt's shop.	acheter, beau, magasin (*m.*), tante (*f.*)
2 The bookshop is closed so I am going home.	librairie (*f.*), fermé, rentrer
3 My brother looks at the nice photos.	frère, regarder, beau, photo (*f.*)
4 Charlotte is going to go for a walk with mum.	se promener, maman
5 They (*m.*) played the piano together this evening.	jouer, piano (*m.*), ensemble, soir

Exercice 9.15

113

Listen to the audio. Five of the six pictures are mentioned. Which ones?

(a)
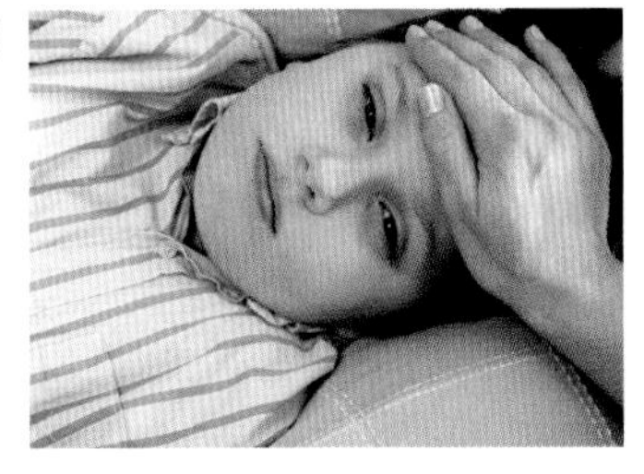

(b)

(c)

(d)

(e)

(f)

En

Les adverbes – Adverbs

A reminder

An adverb tells you more about **how** something is done. The most common way to make an adverb is to take an adjective and add -ment, just as in English we add '-ly':

vrai	true
vraiment	truly, really

To do this, we need a vowel before -ment so, if there isn't one, we use the adjective feminine:

lente	slow
lentement	slowly

Some adverbs used every day are irregular. Here is a shortlist of the prime suspects!

bien	well	trop	too much
vite	quickly	souvent	often
mal	badly	quelquefois	sometimes
mieux	better	longtemps	for a long time
moins bien	not as well	peu	little, not much
pire	worse	toujours	always
encore	again	tous les jours	every day

Exercice 9.16

Prepared talk: A famous artist

Prepare to talk for 30 seconds about a famous artist. Be ready to:

- explain his or her connection with France
- say why you like him or her
- speak a little about one of his or her works.

For example:

Je vais parler de l'artiste Eugène Delacroix. C'est un peintre français né en 1798 à Charenton-Saint-Maurice et mort en 1863 à Paris. Un de ses tableaux s'appelle *La Liberté guidant le peuple*. C'est un tableau important de l'époque napoléonienne.

You need to be ready to answer a few questions about your subject, so research it online in good time. Use the French versions of general information websites.

À la station de ski

In this chapter you'll look at negatives in more detail as well as learning how to compare things.

Exercice 10.1

Read the passage.

Toute la famille a quitté la maison samedi matin à sept heures. Il faisait toujours nuit. En route pour la gare TGV de Nantes, Peter a pu dormir dans la voiture. Tout le monde s'est levé très tôt; personne n'a mangé. Papa a fait du café et on a chargé les bagages dans le coffre de la voiture.

En partant, on a essayé de ne pas faire de bruit, mais ce n'était pas facile. On voyait Madame Demailly qui regardait les allées et venues de derrière la fenêtre de sa salle de bains. Magali était excitée, mais Chloé somnolait: se lever à une heure aussi matinale lui paraissait cruel! Maman conduisait pendant que papa lui indiquait la route. Il n'y avait pas beaucoup de circulation. On roulait en silence. Personne ne parlait ...

On a trouvé le parking longue durée sans problème et maman a garé la voiture, après avoir pris un ticket. Papa a cherché un chariot pour les valises et la famille s'est dirigée vers l'entrée de la gare. Papa a parlé à Peter.

les allées et venues	the comings and goings
une heure aussi matinale	such an early hour
le coffre	the boot (of a car)
somnoler	to doze
le parking longue durée	long-stay car park

paraître cruel	to seem cruel
diriger	to direct
se diriger (vers)	to head (towards), to make one's way (to)
un chariot	a trolley

Answer the questions in English.

1 What happened at seven o'clock that morning?

2 What was the conversation in the car like?

3 What did Chloé think about getting up early on a Saturday morning?

4 What did papa do first when they arrived at the station?

Exercice 10.2

Listen to the audio. Complete each sentence with the correct word.

pratique	practical, convenient
le guichet	ticket office
la borne libre-service	automatic ticket machine
plusieurs	several
tu n'as qu'à ...	all you have to do is ...
l'écran (*m.*)	screen
la correspondance	connection
composter	to validate (a ticket)
la fente	slot
composer un code	to enter a PIN number

1 Papa dit que les machines sont ... (pratiques/difficiles/compliquées)

2 On peut choisir entre aller-retour et aller simple.

3 Ce matin, ... TGVs partent pour Paris. (un/deux/trois)

4 Une correspondance est un changement de ... (car/voiture/train)

5 Les Colbert choisissent le train de ... (8 h 30/9 h 42/11 h 20)

Exercice 10.3

Grammar: focus on verbs

Complete the sentences with the correct version of the verb in brackets in the passé composé.

1	La famille ... en vacances.	partir
2	On ... à la gare à onze heures.	arriver
3	Vous ... bon voyage?	faire
4	Magali et Chloé ... dans la voiture.	dormir
5	Maman ... la carte routière.	regarder

Pour aller plus loin ...

6	Je n'... pas ... de lire le journal.	finir
7	Ils ... le petit-déjeuner dans le train.	prendre
8	À Paris, ils ... prendre le métro.	devoir
9	Papa ... un carnet de tickets.	acheter
10	Tu n'... pas ... les tickets.	oublier

Les expressions négatives – Negative expressions

Here is a full list of negative expressions, to remind you of the ones you have met already and to complete your collection.

ne ... pas	not
ne ... plus	no longer, not any longer, no more
ne ... jamais	never, not ever
ne ... rien	nothing, not anything
ne ... personne	no one, not anyone
ne ... ni ... ni	neither ... nor ...

For example:

Elle ne va jamais au cinéma.	She never goes to the cinema.
On ne porte ni jeans ni baskets ici.	You don't wear jeans or trainers here.

De or *des*?

With negative expressions, de is used (even with plurals), for example:

Je ne mange plus de bananes.	I no longer eat bananas.
Je n'achète jamais de bonbons.	I never buy sweets.

But with ne … que ('only'), which is not really a negative, we use des, for example:

Maman n'a acheté que des fruits au marché.	Mum only bought fruit at the market.
Je n'ai que des bonbons.	I only have sweets.

Negative expressions in the passé composé

When using these negative expressions with verbs in the perfect, simply make the avoir or être part negative, then add the participe passé:

Elle n'a rien vu.	She hasn't seen anything.
On n'a pas mangé.	We haven't eaten.
Il n'est jamais venu chez moi.	He has never come to my house.

No one is a special case!

Personne and rien can be both the subject and object in a sentence.

On n'a trouvé personne à la piscine.	We found no one at the swimming pool.
Personne ne m'a vu.	No one saw me.
Rien n'est arrivé.	Nothing happened.

Notice how these expressions appear to be double negatives.

Exercice 10.4

Rewrite these sentences with the negative expression shown.

Remember that after a negative, we don't say du, de la, de l' or des; we say de.

1 Magali a grimpé aux arbres.	pas
2 Maman a pris des photos.	jamais
3 Jérôme et moi avons promené le chien.	pas
4 Il y a de la neige.	plus
5 On sait.	jamais

Pour aller plus loin ...

Here, it's up to you to get the right negative word!

6	Tu as fini ton repas?	not
7	Ils arrivent à temps.	never
8	Vous allez partir dans trois minutes!	not
9	... a sorti les poubelles aujourd'hui!	no one
10	Je ... ai ... vu sur le quai de la gare.	nothing

Exercice 10.5

Listen to the audio. Answer the questions in English

la journée	day
entier (*f.* entière)	whole
rondelet	round, plump
enchanté(e)	delighted
s'installer	to settle in
la minuterie	timed light for stairways and dark corridors
par ici	this way
se dépêcher	to hurry
à emporter	to take away
de ce côté	on this side
le palier	landing

1 How long did the journey take from home to the ski resort?

2 Describe the weather and light conditions when they arrived.

3 Who let them into the chalet?

4 What does papa ask?

5 When did Magali lose her watch?

6 Why do you think Chloé is so hungry?

7 Why was it a bad idea to go to a restaurant?

8 What did they decide to eat?

Exercice 10.6

Translate:

1 We (On) arrived at seven p.m., when it was already dark.	dix-neuf heures, faire nuit
2 You could see snowflake were.	voir, flocon (*m.*) de neige
3 My friend (*f.*), who has not slept in the car, is very tired.	copine (*f.*), dormir, voiture (*f.*), fatigué
4 My brother was reading the map, but it was difficult.	frère, lire, carte (*f.*) routière, difficile
5 He could not see very well and we had to ask the way.	voir, devoir, demander, chemin (*m.*)

Exercice 10.7

Complete with the correct word for 'to the' or 'at the':

1 La famille est arrivée … gare (*f.*).

2 … parking (*m.*), on a vite trouvé une place.

3 Martine a couru … escalier.

4 On est descendus … arrêt d'autobus.

5 … station de métro, on a acheté un carnet.

Pour aller plus loin ...

6 Tu veux aller ... magasins?

7 Magali est allée … banque (*f.*) avec maman.

8 … école, j'apprends à parler anglais.

9 J'aimerais monter … Tour (*f.*) Eiffel.

10 Rendez-vous … Arc de Triomphe!

Exercice 10.8

Read this passage and try to understand it. You can also read it aloud for pronunciation practice.

Peter était débutant, c'est-à-dire que c'était la première fois qu'il allait faire du ski. Le matin de sa première sortie sur les pistes, il a posé beaucoup de questions à Magali et à ses parents. Au petit-déjeuner, il était trop impatient pour manger!

Les Colbert et Peter sont sortis du chalet vers neuf heures du matin. Pendant la nuit il neigeait et tout était couvert d'une couche de neige poudreuse. La montagne était encore plus belle que d'habitude et la neige scintillait dans les sapins. Maman et papa ont regardé un petit plan des environs de la ville et sont allés à pied au magasin de sports.

Papa a loué tout le nécessaire: des skis, des chaussures de ski et des bâtons, et il a acheté une salopette et des gants pour Peter qui n'en avait pas. Puis ils sont tous allés sur les pistes et ont fait la queue pour acheter des ski-pass pour le remonte-pente. Papa, maman et Magali sont partis sur une piste rouge, car ils étaient des skieurs expérimentés, tandis que Chloé a accompagné Peter à l'école de ski.

Il y avait deux moniteurs et une monitrice. Chloé a tout expliqué à un moniteur qui les a mis dans un groupe de dix débutants et débutantes.

le/la débutant(e)	beginner
la sortie	outing
la piste*	ski run
la couche	layer
poudreux (*f.* poudreuse)	powdery
le sapin	fir tree
scintiller	to sparkle

la chaussure de ski	ski boot
le bâton de ski	ski pole
la salopette	salopette
le gant	glove
expérimenté(e)	experienced
le remonte-pente	ski lift
tandis que	while
le moniteur	instructor (*m.*)
la monitrice	instructor (*f.*)
rassembler	to assemble, to bring together

* la piste also means a track or a runway

La comparaison – Comparison

Comparing people or things using adjectives

Remember that to make comparisons – comparing people and things – we use the following expressions:

plus (adjectif) que	more (adjective) than
moins (adjectif) que	less (adjective) than
aussi (adjectif) que	as (adjective) as

Don't forget that we still need to make the adjective agree with the noun or pronoun it describes, for example:

Sophie est plus intelligent**e** que Charles.

Les frères de Marie sont aussi fort**s** que leurs cousins.

Les comparatifs irréguliers de certains adjectifs

Some adjectives have irregular comparatives:

bon	good	mauvais	bad
meilleur	better	pire	worse

Comparison of adverbs

Adverbs are used in comparing, like adjectives. Just as we can say 'he is taller than Paul', so we can say 'she skis better than Sophie'. In the second example, the word 'better' describes the verb 'skis', so it is an adverb.

plus (adverbe) que	more (adverb) than
moins (adverbe) que	less (adverb) than
aussi (adverbe) que	as (adverb) as

Adverbs do not 'agree'; they are invariable, for example:

Elle skie plus vite que sa sœur.

There are a few irregulars, which we use a lot.

Some adverbs also have irregular comparatives:

bien	well	mieux	better
mal	badly	moins	less
peu	little		

Exercice 10.9

Using the adjectives in the box below to help you, give the French for:

1 bigger than (*f.*)
2 smaller than (*m.*)
3 as intelligent (*m. pl.*) as
4 more talkative (*f.*) than
5 shorter (*m.*) than
6 more dangerous (*f.*) than
7 lower (*m.*) than
8 more slippery (*m. pl.*) than

9 less useful (*f. pl.*) than

10 as practical (*m.*) as

low	bas (*f.* basse)	talkative	bavard
slippery	glissant	short	court
useful	utile	dangerous	dangereux (*f.* dangereuse)
practical	pratique		

Exercice 10.10

Role play: À l'école de ski

You (A) are at a ski-school speaking with a moniteur/monitrice (B).

Take it in turns to be A and B.

A. Hello. Is this Class 2?

B. Oui, c'est ça. Tu t'appelles comment?

A. [Answer the question.]

B. Bon, d'abord, on va apprendre le chasse-neige.

A. It's better than last time!

B. J'espère bien!

A. Is it difficult?

B. C'est la première fois que tu fais du ski?

A. No, it's the second time.

B. Alors non, ça va être facile pour toi.

Exercice 10.11

Prepared talk: A historical figure

Prepare to talk for 30 seconds on a historical figure. Be ready to:

- explain his or her connection with France
- say why you like him or her
- speak a little about why he or she is famous.

For example:

Je vais parler de Napoléon. Napoléon 1er est né en 1769 à Ajaccio, en Corse, et mort en 1821 à Sainte-Hélène. C'est le premier empereur de France. Un grand stratège militaire, il est devenu célèbre après la Révolution française …

You need to be ready to answer a few questions about your subject, so research it online in good time. Use the French versions of general information websites.

Exercice 10.12

La boîte en argent (suite et fin)

This audio and reading passage concludes the story of the little silver box. Listen to the audio while reading the text and then discuss as a class the era of the Occupation and its effect on France.

Magali, Chloé et Peter ont passé une semaine inoubliable à faire du ski dans les Alpes. De retour à La Roche-sur-Yon, tout le monde est fatigué mais très content. Les filles commencent à penser aux vacances de Noël et Peter se met à préparer ses bagages pour rentrer en Angleterre.

Après le dîner à la maison, les filles racontent l'histoire de la petite boîte en argent que Madame Demailly a trouvée dans son jardin cet été.

Maman met une lettre sur la table. Tout le monde la regarde.

Chloé. C'est quoi, maman? Ça ressemble à l'écriture de Mamie.

Maman. C'est exact! J'ai reçu la lettre avant d'aller en vacances.

Magali. Pourquoi tu n'as rien dit?

Maman. J'avais peur. C'était peut-être de mauvaises nouvelles … Je ne voulais pas l'ouvrir avant de partir.

Chloé. Alors?

Maman. J'avais tort! Elle a tout résolu! Je vais vous lire un extrait de la lettre:

> […] donc je voulais que la lettre arrive avant votre retour à la maison. D'abord, non seulement Monsieur Jean-Paul Lévy habitait ici, mais … il n'est pas mort! Il a 87 ans et il a reçu la boîte en argent en 1944 pour son anniversaire. Le lendemain, des soldats sont venus dans sa maison et ont enlevé toute la famille. Ils ont été déportés et les parents n'ont pas survécu.
>
> Mais Jean-Paul, âgé de 14 ans à l'époque, vit toujours! Il habite à Bordeaux. J'ai son adresse!
>
> […]

Maman.	Et ainsi de suite. L'amie d'enfance de Mamie a fait toutes les recherches.
Chloé.	C'est incroyable! On va finalement pouvoir rendre la petite boîte à son propriétaire!
Magali.	Mais il faut fêter ça! On va inviter Mme Demailly et tous nos amis et présenter la boîte à Jean-Paul! On pourrait le faire à Noël!
Peter.	Quelle belle histoire! C'est dommage mais je vais être chez moi.
Papa.	Si tu veux, tu peux rester pour Noël ...
Peter.	Vraiment? Mais ...
Papa.	Il neige sur Paris. Les avions ne décollent pas ... et puis j'ai téléphoné à tes parents ...

et ainsi de suite	and so on
à l'époque	at the time; at that time

Exercice 10.13

In the passage from Exercice 10.12, find the French expressions that mean:

1. it looks like the handwriting
2. bad news
3. before leaving
4. I was wrong
5. and so on
6. the childhood friend
7. the planes aren't taking off

Show you can adapt an expression to fit what you want to say:

8	it looks like the exercise book	cahier (*m.*)
9	good food	cuisine (*f.*) – 'food' in this sense means 'cooking', of course
10	before arriving	
11	she was right	avoir raison
12	the ferries aren't leaving the port	ferry (*m.*), quitter, port (*m.*)

Exercice 10.14

Translate:

1 My mother found the letter when she arrived.	mère (*f.*), trouver, lettre (*f.*), arriver
2 They (*f.*) were quite tired but happy to be at home.	fatigué, content (de + *infin.*), maison (*f.*)
3 The young people enjoyed themselves	jeunes gens (*m.pl.*), s'amuser
4 Why don't we play tennis this afternoon?	jouer, tennis (*m.*), après-midi
5 Our house's doors are not grey, they are white.	porte (*f.*), gris, blanc (*f.* blanche)

Exercice 10.15

Write an email in French to your French teacher, in which you tell him/her about your holidays. Write 80–120 words. You must mention four of the following five points:

• where you are now	où tu te trouves maintenant
• a place you have visited	une visite que tu as faite
• a meal you enjoyed	un repas que tu as aimé
• a new friend	un(e) nouvel(le) ami(e)
• how you are travelling home	comment tu vas rentrer à la maison

Don't forget to add description to make your email more interesting (and get higher marks!).

G Grammar

Where to look things up

Grammar summary

1 You – Choosing the right word for 'you'

tu	is for a young person of your age, a member of your family or a pet.
vous	is for any adult you don't know well (a teacher, shopkeeper, etc.) or for more than one person.

Adults use vous for speaking to another adult until they know him or her well.

2 The – How to say 'the'

le	is for a masculine noun in the singular	le disque
la	is for a feminine noun in the singular	la radio
l'	is for a singular noun beginning with a vowel or silent 'h' except some words (the dictionary tells you which ones), which keep le or la	l'école, l'hôtel la haie*, le héros*
les	is for all plural nouns	les vélos

* la haie = the hedge; le héros = the hero.

In these words, we do not pronounce the 'h' in the English way, but the words are treated in every other way as though we did.

3 A (an) – How to say 'a'

un	is for a masculine noun	un hôtel
une	is for a feminine noun	une forêt

4 Some/any – How to say 'some' or 'any'

du	is for a masculine noun in the singular	du lait
de la	is for a feminine noun in the singular	de la salade
de l'	is for a singular noun beginning with a vowel or silent 'h'	de l'argent
des	is for all plural nouns	des oranges

Note that in English we often leave out the word 'some'; it is never left out in French:

e.g. You have (some) books and pencils. = Tu as des livres et des crayons.

5 Plurals – How to make nouns plural

To make a noun plural, we usually just add -s:	un livre, des livres
Nouns ending in -eau add -x:	un cadeau, des cadeaux
Most nouns ending in -al generally change -al to -aux:	un cheval, des chevaux

6 My – Choosing the right word for 'my'

'My' followed by a masculine singular noun is mon:

mon livre = my book

'My' followed by a feminine singular noun is usually ma:

ma sœur = my sister

However, 'my' followed by a feminine noun beginning with a vowel or silent 'h' is mon:

mon amie = my friend (*f.*)

'My' followed by any plural noun is mes:

mes livres = my books

7 Your (when using tu) – How to choose the right word for 'your'

The words for 'your', ton, ta, tes, work in exactly the same way as mon, ma, mes:

ton livre = your book

ta sœur = your sister, but ton amie = your friend (*f.*)

tes livres = your books

The word for 'your' followed by a feminine noun beginning with a vowel or silent 'h' is ton:

ton amie = your friend (*f.*).

8 His/her and their – How to choose the right word

The word for 'his' and 'her' is the same in French, regardless of whether the 'owner' is male or female:

When followed by a masculine noun, it is son:

son livre = his/her book.

The word for 'his' or 'her' followed by a feminine noun is sa:

sa sœur = his/her sister.

The word for 'his' or 'her' with a plural noun is ses:

ses parents = his/her parents.

The word for 'his' or 'her' followed by a feminine noun beginning with a vowel or silent 'h' is son:

son amie = his/her friend (*f.*).

The word for 'their' is leur (singular) and leurs (plural). It is the same for masculine and feminine nouns:

f.: leur bicyclette = their bicycle	leurs bicyclettes = their bicycles
m.: leur garage = their garage	leurs garages = their garages

9 Your (when using vous) – How to choose the right word for 'your'

votre with a singular noun, either masculine or feminine, e.g. votre vélo

vos with a plural noun, e.g. vos vélos

10 Here is, there is – How to say 'here is/are' and 'there is/are'

When pointing to things:

voici here is/here are

voilà there is/there are (N.B. voilà! also means: 'there you are!')

e.g. Voilà un chien. = There is a dog (over there).

But when giving information:

il y a there is/there are

e.g. Il y a un chien dans le jardin. = There is a dog in the garden.

e.g. Il y a des araignées dans ma chambre. = There are spiders in my bedroom.

11 How to say 'not' – Basic negative and other negative expressions

Put ne before the verb and pas after it:

Je ne sais pas = I do **not** know/I do**n't** know

If there is an infinitive, put ne and pas around the verb *before* the infinitive:

Je ne vais pas chanter = I am **not** going to sing

More negative expressions:

ne ... plus	no longer, not any longer, no more
ne ... jamais	never, not ever
ne ... rien	nothing, not anything
ne ... personne	no one, not anyone

Most of these negative expressions are used in the same way as ne ... pas:

Je ne mange plus de bananes.	I no longer eat bananas.
Elle ne va jamais au cinéma.	She never goes to the cinema.
On ne porte ni jeans ni baskets ici.	We don't wear jeans or trainers here.

> Reminder: In a sentence involving a plural noun, ne ... que (= only), which is not really a negative expression, is followed by des.

Example:

Maman n'achète que des fruits.	Mum only buys fruit.

Personne and rien may be used as the subject of a sentence. Note the word order:

Personne ne vient me voir.	No one comes to see me.
Rien n'arrive ici.	Nothing happens here.

In the passé composé, the auxiliary verb is made negative and then the past participle is added:

Elle n'a rien vu.	She hasn't seen anything.
On n'avait pas mangé.	We hadn't eaten.
Tu n'es plus venu chez moi.	You didn't come to my house any more.

With formations using the infinitive, only the verb preceding the infinitive is made negative:

On ne va plus aller au parc.	We're not going to go to the park any more.

12 Adjectives – All you need to know about adjectives

Adjectives are 'describing' words. In French, they must agree with the noun they describe. Most are put *after* the noun.

The basic adjective is masculine singular	un crayon vert
To make it feminine, you normally just add an -e	une table verte
To make it plural, you normally just add an -s	des crayons verts
To make it feminine plural, add BOTH -e and -s	des tables vertes

Some have their own special (irregular) forms:

Masculine	Masculine + vowel	Feminine	Plural
beau	bel	belle	beaux/belles
nouveau	nouvel	nouvelle	nouveaux/ nouvelles
blanc		blanche	blancs/ blanches
vieux	vieil	vieille	vieux/vieilles
doux		douce	doux/douces

Note also:

gentil	gentille
bon	bonne
actif	active

Note that several adjectives come before the noun. To help you remember which, remember BAGS:

Examples:

B	Beauty	beau, joli, vilain
A	Age	jeune, vieux
G	Goodness	bon, mauvais, méchant
S	Size	grand, petit, haut, gros

Adjectives describing any of these usually go before the noun.

There is more about adjectives in Book 1, Chapitre 5.

13 Questions – How to make questions

There are 3 ways to ask a question:

1 Reverse the order of person and verb (inversion)
2 Put Est-ce que... before the sentence, without changing anything else
3 Use your tone of voice (intonation).

Examples:

Veux-tu un bonbon?

Est-ce que tu veux un bonbon?

Tu veux un bonbon?

Questions words: a reminder

qui?	who?
que?	what?
qu'est-ce que?	what? (+ verb expression, e.g. what are you doing?)
comment?	how?
quand?	when?
pourquoi?	why?
où?	where?
combien (de)?	how many? how much?
quel, quelle, quels, quelles (+ noun)?	which ...? what ...?

Attention! qui is never shortened, but que becomes qu' before a vowel or silent 'h'.

14 To/at + the; of/from + the – How to say 'to', 'at', 'of' and 'from' with 'the'

We do NOT say	à le **or** à les,		de le **or** de les	
Instead we say	au	aux	du	des

(a) à can mean 'to' or 'at'. To say 'to the...' or 'to/at the...':

m.	au cinéma = to/at the cinema
f.	à la piscine = to/at the swimming pool
vowel or silent 'h'	à l'homme = to the man; à l'école = to/at (the) school

The French for 'to the' or 'at the', followed by any plural noun, is aux:

aux magasins = to/at the shops

(b) de can mean 'of' or 'from'. To say 'of the...' or 'from the...':

m.	du cinéma = of/from the cinema
f.	de la piscine = of/from the swimming pool
vowel or silent 'h'	de l'homme = of/from the man; de l'école = of/from (the) school

The French for 'of the' or 'from the', followed by any plural noun, is des:

des magasins = of the shops/from the shops

15 Going to do – The future tense, using aller + infinitive

To talk about things that are going to happen, use the present tense of aller, then add the infinitive of whatever is going to happen:

je vais vendre = I am going to sell

16 Activities – Choosing between aller, faire and jouer

The French for 'to play' is jouer. Jouer is regularly followed by au:

jouer au tennis = to play tennis

jouer au ping-pong = to play table tennis

The French for 'to go' is aller:

aller à la pêche = to go fishing

However, for several activities where in English we use the verb 'to go', in French the verb faire is used:

faire du cheval = to go riding

faire du ski = to go skiing

faire un pique-nique = to go for a picnic

faire une promenade = to go for a walk

17 Prepositions – Position words

A preposition is a word that tells us where something is in relation to something else:

dans = in

derrière = behind

devant = in front of

à côté de = beside, next to

à gauche de = to the left of

à droite de = to the right of

sur = on

sous = under

entre = between

en face de = opposite

18 Joining words – Conjunctions

A conjunction is a word that links ideas together in a sentence:

mais = but	parce que = because
si = if	car = for, because
et = and	ou = or

19 Time and weather – Talking about time and weather

Weather

Many weather expressions use the verb faire:

Il fait beau. = It's fine.

Il fait chaud. = It is hot.

There are other weather verbs:

infinitif	présent
neiger (to snow, to be snowing)	il neige
pleuvoir (to rain, to be raining)	il pleut
geler (to freeze, to be freezing)	il gèle

Asking about the weather:

Quel temps fait-il? = What is the weather like?

Time

For telling the time we use the 24-hour clock and il est for 'it is'.

What's the time?/What time is it?	Quelle heure est-il?
It's three o'clock	Il est trois heures
It's three in the afternoon/3 p.m.	Il est quinze heures/15 h
It's ten past five/5.10	Il est cinq heures dix/5 h 10
It's a quarter past three/3.15	Il est trois heures et quart
It's half past two/2.30	Il est deux heures et demie
It's twenty to eleven	Il est onze heures moins vingt
It's a quarter to eleven	Il est onze heures moins le quart
It's ten to eleven	Il est onze heures moins dix
It's midday/12 p.m.	Il est midi/12 h
It's midnight/12 a.m.	Il est minuit/24 h

20 To and in + place – How to say 'to' or 'in' with towns, cities and countries

Towns

For all cities, towns or villages, of any size, use à:

à Paris = to Paris; in Paris

Countries

For countries with feminine names (mostly those ending in e), use en:

en France = to France; in France

For countries with masculine names, use au:

au Canada = to Canada; in Canada

au Maroc = to Morocco; in Morocco

au Japon = to Japan; in Japan

au Portugal = to Portugal; in Portugal

au Sénégal = to Senegal; in Senegal

Countries with plural names take aux:

aux États-Unis = to the USA; in the USA

21 This/that + thing/person – How to say 'this', 'that', 'these' and 'those'

All the singular words mean *this* or *that*. The plural means *these* or *those*:

	singular	plural
m.	ce	ces
m. (before a vowel or silent 'h')	cet	ces
f.	cette	ces

22 Avoir idioms – Expressions with avoir

Avoir is used in many French expressions where English uses the verb 'to be':

avoir l'air - to seem; to appear to be

avoir besoin de = to need

avoir chaud = to be hot

avoir envie de = to want

avoir faim = to be hungry

avoir lieu = to take place

avoir peur = to be afraid

avoir raison = to be right

avoir soif = to be thirsty

avoir sommeil = to be sleepy

avoir froid = to be cold

avoir tort = to be wrong

avoir honte = to be ashamed

23 Pronouns – Words we use to avoid repeating nouns

subject (I, etc.)	direct object (me, etc.)	reflexive (myself, etc.)
je	me	me
tu	te	te
il	le	se
elle	la	se
on		se
nous	nous	nous
vous	vous	vous
ils	les	se
elles	les	se

Some special pronouns are used alone or after a preposition, as in this example in English:

A Who had salad for lunch?

B Me!

And in French:

A Qui a mangé les croissants?

B Moi!

Here are all the special (so-called 'strong') pronouns:

moi me

toi you (*sing.*)

lui him

elle her

nous us

vous you (*pl.*)

eux them (*m.*)

elles them (*f.*)

24 Imperatives (commands) – Telling people what to do

To make the 'command' form of a verb, take either the second person singular or second person plural of the verb, removing tu or vous:

Tu descends. = You go down.	>	Descends! = Go down!
Vous descendez.	>	Descendez!

On -ER verbs, remove the -s from the second person singular ending:

Tu parles. – You are speaking.	>	Parle! = Speak!

Commands using reflexive ('selfie') verbs

Do the same as for a normal verb (see above) but add -toi or -vous as appropriate:

Tu te lèves. = You get up.	>	Lève-toi! = Get up!
Vous vous levez.	>	Levez-vous!

25 Comparison – How to make comparisons

The following are used to form comparisons:

plus	[adjectif]	que	more	[adjective]	than
moins	[adjectif]	que	less	[adjective]	than
aussi	[adjectif]	que	as	[adjective]	as

Le film est **plus** drôle **que** le livre. The film is funnier than the book.

The adjective needs to agree with the pronoun it describes:

Sophie est plus intelligente que son frère. = Sophie is more intelligent than her brother.

Les frères de Pierre sont aussi forts que ses cousins. = Pierre's brothers are as strong as his cousins.

The same rules also apply for adverbs (see section 'Adverbs'), though they do not have to agree:

plus	[adverbe]	que	more	[adverb]	than
moins	[adverbe]	que	less	[adverb]	than
aussi	[adverbe]	que	as	[adverb]	as

Elle skie **plus** vite **que** sa sœur.

26 Adverbs – All you need to know about adverbs

Usually an adverb is formed by adding the suffix -ment to the corresponding adjective, rather like adding -ly to 'quick' to make 'quickly' in English:

vrai	(true)	vraiment	(truly, really)
facile	(easy)	facilement	(easily)

There needs to be a vowel before -ment, so, if there isn't, use the feminine adjective:

lent	(slow)	lent**e**ment	(slowly)

Some commonly used adverbs are irregular and not formed in this way:

bientôt	soon	encore	again
quelquefois	sometimes	peu	little, not much
souvent	often	toujours	always
pire	worse		

27 That – Choosing the right word for 'that'

When trying to find the right French word for 'that', consider these examples:

That house is small	Cette maison est petite	(from ce, cet, cette, ces)
Do you see that?	Tu vois ça?	(ça = it or that)
He says that Paul is French	Il dit que Paul est français	

Stop to think which example is the one you need.

28 Which – Choosing the right word for 'which'

When trying to find the right French word for 'which', consider these examples:

Which film are you going to see?	Tu vas voir quel film?	(from quel, quels, quelle, quelles)
The book which you like	Le livre que tu aimes	(referring to the noun before *it*)

Stop to think which example is the one you need.

29 Who – Choosing the right word for 'who'

When trying to find the right French word for 'who', consider these examples:

Who has the answer?	Qui a la réponse?	(question word)
The girl who lives here	La fille qui habite ici	(subject of verb)
The man who(m) I know	L'homme **que** je connais	(object of verb)

Stop to think which example is the one you need.

30 – Verbs

a) The meanings of each tense

- Present Présent

  Elle regarde = She watches/She is watching

- Present perfect tense Passé composé

  Elle a regardé. = She watched./She has watched.

- Imperfect Imparfait

  Elle regardait. = She was watching./She used to watch.

- Perfect Passé composé

  Elle a regardé. = She watched.

- Near future Futur proche

  Elle va regarder. = She is going to watch.

- Conditional Conditionnel

  Elle regarderait. = She would watch.

  Je voudrais = I would like

b) How to form each tense

- **Present tense**

The present tenses of regular verbs are shown in the tables below. Regular verbs follow patterns of stem + ending, but each irregular verb must be learnt individually from the Verb tables that follow this section.

- Perfect tense Le passé composé

The passé composé is made from avoir or être, in the present tense, and a past participle:

J'ai fini. = I have finished/I finished. (Most verbs take avoir in the passé composé)

Je suis parti. = I have left/I left.

The following verbs take être in the passé composé. Note that after such verbs, **all** past participles must agree with the subject: elle est partie, ils sont partis, elles sont parties. So a girl would say je suis partie.

aller (allé) (*irregular*) = to go
entrer (entré) = to go in
arriver (arrivé) = to arrive
monter (monté) = to go up
rester (resté) = to stay
rentrer (rentré) = to come home
naître (né) (*irregular*) = to be born
devenir (devenu) (*irregular*) = to become
venir (venu) (*irregular*) = to come
sortir (sorti) (*irregular*) = to go out
partir (parti) (*irregular*) = to leave
descendre (descendu) = to go down
tomber (tombé) = to fall
retourner (retourné) = to return
mourir (mort) (*irregular*) = to die
revenir (revenu) (*irregular*) = to come back, return

Negatives and questions in the passé composé

To form a negative or a question in the passé composé, make any changes to avoir or être.

The past participle remains unchanged:

	Negative	**Question**
Tu as regardé.	Tu n'as pas regardé.	As-tu regardé?
Il a regardé.	Il n'a pas regardé.	A-t-il regardé?

- **Imperfect tense** L'imparfait

The imparfait is made from the nous part of the present tense, without the ending -ons.

nous prenons: pren-

The following endings are then added to this stem:

je	-ais	je prenais
tu	-ais	tu prenais
il	-ait	il prenait
elle	-ait	elle prenait
nous	-ions	nous prenions
vous	-iez	vous preniez
ils	-aient	ils prenaient
elles	-aient	elles prenaient

The only verb that has an irregular stem is être, whose stem is ét-:

j'étais c'était

- **Near future** Le futur proche

The futur proche is made by using the present tense of aller before an infinitive:

je **vais** regarder	I am going to watch	nous **allons** regarder	we are going to watch
tu **vas** regarder	you are going to watch	vous **allez** regarder	you are going to watch
il **va** regarder	he is going to watch	ils **vont** regarder	they are going to watch
elle **va** regarder	she is going to watch	elles **vont** regarder	they are going to watch

- **Conditional: the 'would' tense**

The conditional tense of a verb is the one that means 'would'.

For CE, you only need to know two conditional expressions:

je voudrais	I would like (from vouloir, to want)
j'aimerais	I would like (from aimer, to like)

Examples: Je voudrais un kilo de pommes — I would like a kilo of apples

J'aimerais aller au cinéma — I would like to go to the cinema

c) Reflexive ('selfie') verbs

Reflexive verbs are verbs that you 'do to yourself', like taking a selfie.

They are the same as normal verbs, except that you have to put a 'self' word before the verb:

Elle regarde. = She looks. Elle se regarde. = She looks at herself (e.g. in the mirror).

The 'self' words are:

me	myself	nous	ourselves
te	yourself	vous	yourself/yourselves
se	himself	se	themselves (*m.* or *f.*)
se	herself		
se	oneself		

Example: nous nous lavons = we wash ourselves

ALL reflexive verbs take être in the passé composé. Note the word order:

elles se sont levées	nous nous sommes levé(e)s
tu t'es levé(e)	vous vous êtes levé(e)(s)
il s'est levé	ils se sont levés
elle s'est levée	elles se sont levées

Verb tables

1 Regular verbs

Present tense

All regular verbs belong to one of three groups: -ER (1st group), -IR (2nd group) and -RE (3rd group). The endings to each verb are different depending on which group they are in. This applies to all tenses, but is most obvious in the present:

1st group: -ER

regarder: to watch, look at					
je	regard-e	I watch	nous	regard-ons	we watch
tu	regard-es	you watch	vous	regard-ez	you watch
il	regard-e	he watches	ils	regard-ent	they watch
elle	regard-e	she watches	elles	regard-ent	they watch

2nd group: -IR

finir: to finish					
je	fin-is	I finish	nous	fin-issons	we finish
tu	fin-is	you finish	vous	fin-issez	you finish
il	fin-it	he finishes	ils	fin-issent	they finish
elle	fin-it	she finishes	elles	fin-issent	they finish

3rd group: -RE

vendre: to sell					
je	vend-s	I sell	nous	vend-ons	we sell
tu	vend-s	you sell	vous	vend-ez	you sell
il	vend	he sells	ils	vend-ent	they sell
elle	vend	she sells	elles	vend-ent	they sell

2 Reflexive verbs

Here is a reflexive verb set out in full:

se laver: to wash (oneself)			
je me lave	I wash (myself)	nous nous lavons	we wash (ourselves)
tu te laves	you wash (yourself)	vous vous lavez	you wash (yourselves)
il se lave	he washes (himself)	ils se lavent	they wash (themselves)
elle se lave	she washes (herself)	elles se lavent	they wash (themselves)

Any verb can be made reflexive, as long as it makes sense!

Je lave le chien. = I wash the dog.

Je me lave. = I wash (myself).

Near future (le futur proche)

The futur proche is made by using the present tense of aller before an infinitive:

je **vais** regarder	I am going to watch	nous **allons** regarder	we are going to watch
tu **vas** regarder	you are going to watch	vous **allez** regarder	you are going to watch
il **va** regarder	he is going to watch	ils **vont** regarder	they are going to watch
elle **va** regarder	she is going to watch	elles **vont** regarder	they are going to watch

3 Irregular verbs

Irregular verbs are those that do not follow the patterns of the three main groups. They are often the most commonly used. Verbs with an asterisk (*) take être in the passé composé.

présent | **passé composé**

acheter: to buy (è/e)	
j'achète	nous achetons
tu achètes	vous achetez
il achète	ils achètent
elle achète	elles achètent
on achète	

j'ai acheté
(avoir + acheté)

aller*: to go	
je vais	nous allons
tu vas	vous allez
il va	ils vont
elle va	elles vont
on va	

je suis allé(e)
(être + allé)

appeler: to call (ll/l)	
j'appelle	nous appelons
tu appelles	vous appelez
il appelle	ils appellent
elle appelle	elles appellent
on appelle	

j'ai appelé
(avoir + appelé)

présent		passé composé
s'asseoir: to sit down		je me suis assis(e) (être + assis)
je m'assieds	nous nous asseyons	
tu t'assieds	vous vous asseyez	
il s'assied	ils s'asseyent	
elle s'assied	elles s'asseyent	
on s'assied		
avoir: to have		j'ai eu (avoir + eu)
j'ai	nous avons	
tu as	vous avez	
il a	ils ont	
elle a	elles ont	
on a		
battre: to beat		j'ai battu (avoir + battu)
je bats	nous battons	
tu bats	vous battez	
il bat	ils battent	
elle bat	elles battent	
on bat		
boire: to drink		j'ai bu (avoir + bu)
je bois	nous buvons	
tu bois	vous buvez	
il boit	ils boivent	
elle boit	elles boivent	
on boit		
connaître: to know (a person or place)		j'ai connu (avoir + connu)
je connais	nous connaissons	
tu connais	vous connaissez	
il connaît	ils connaissent	
elle connaît	elles connaissent	
on connaît		

présent		passé composé

courir: to run		
je cours	nous courons	j'ai couru (avoir + couru)
tu cours	vous courez	
il court	ils courent	
elle court	elles courent	
on court		

croire: to believe		
je crois	nous croyons	j'ai cru (avoir + cru)
tu crois	vous croyez	
il croit	ils croient	
elle croit	elles croient	
on croit		

devoir: to have to, to owe		
je dois	nous devons	j'ai dû (avoir + dû)
tu dois	vous devez	
il doit	ils doivent	
elle doit	elles doivent	
on doit		

dire: to say		
je dis	nous disons	j'ai dit (avoir + dit)
tu dis	vous dites	
il dit	ils disent	
elle dit	elles disent	
on dit		

dormir: to sleep		
je dors	nous dormons	j'ai dormi (avoir + dormi)
tu dors	vous dormez	
il dort	ils dorment	
elle dort	elles dorment	
on dort		

présent | **passé composé**

écrire: to write		passé composé
j'écris	nous écrivons	j'ai écrit (avoir + écrit)
tu écris	vous écrivez	
il écrit	ils écrivent	
elle écrit	elles écrivent	
on écrit		

envoyer: to send (i/y)		passé composé
j'envoie	nous envoyons	j'ai envoyé (avoir + envoyé)
tu envoies	vous envoyez	
il envoie	ils envoient	
elle envoie	elles envoient	
on envoie		

essayer: to try		passé composé
j'essaie	nous essayons	j'ai essayé (avoir + essayé)
tu essaies	vous essayez	
il essaie	ils essaient	
elle essaie	elles essaient	
on essaie		

être: to be		passé composé
je suis	nous sommes	j'ai été (avoir + été)
tu es	vous êtes	
il est	ils sont	
elle est	elles sont	
on est		

faire: to do; to make		passé composé
je fais	nous faisons	j'ai fait (avoir + fait)
tu fais	vous faites	
il fait	ils font	
elle fait	elles font	
on fait		

présent		passé composé
falloir: to be necessary (only used with il)		il a fallu (avoir + fallu)
il faut		

jeter: to throw (tt/t)		j'ai jeté (avoir + jeté)
je jette	nous jetons	
tu jettes	vous jetez	
il jette	ils jettent	
elle jette	elles jettent	
on jette		

lire: to read		j'ai lu (avoir + lu)
je lis	nous lisons	
tu lis	vous lisez	
il lit	ils lisent	
elle lit	elles lisent	
on lit		

mener: to lead (è/e)		j'ai mené (avoir + mené)
je mène	nous menons	
tu mènes	vous menez	
il mène	ils mènent	
elle mène	elles mènent	
on mène		

mettre: to put, to put on		j'ai mis (avoir + mis)
je mets	nous mettons	
tu mets	vous mettez	
il met	ils mettent	
elle met	elles mettent	
on met		

présent		passé composé
mourir*: to die		je suis mort(e) (être + mort)
je meurs	nous mourons	
tu meurs	vous mourez	
il meurt	ils meurent	
elle meurt	elles meurent	
on meurt		
naître*: to be born		je suis né(e) (être + né)
je nais	nous naissons	
tu nais	vous naissez	
il naît	ils naissent	
elle naît	elles naissent	
on naît		
ouvrir: to open		j'ai ouvert (avoir + ouvert)
j'ouvre	nous ouvrons	
tu ouvres	vous ouvrez	
il ouvre	ils ouvrent	
elle ouvre	elles ouvrent	
on ouvre		
partir*: to leave		je suis parti(e) (être + parti)
je pars	nous partons	
tu pars	vous partez	
il part	ils partent	
elle part	elles partent	
on part		
pouvoir: to be able to		j'ai pu (avoir + pu)
je peux	nous pouvons	
tu peux	vous pouvez	
il peut	ils peuvent	
elle peut	elles peuvent	
on peut		

présent		passé composé
prendre: to take		j'ai pris (avoir + pris)
je prends	nous prenons	
tu prends	vous prenez	
il prend	ils prennent	
elle prend	elles prennent	
on prend		

recevoir: to receive		j'ai reçu (avoir + reçu)
je reçois	nous recevons	
tu reçois	vous recevez	
il reçoit	ils reçoivent	
elle reçoit	elles reçoivent	
on reçoit		

rire: to laugh		j'ai ri (avoir + ri)
je ris	nous rions	
tu ris	vous riez	
il rit	ils rient	
elle rit	elles rient	
on rit		

savoir: to know		j'ai su (avoir + su)
je sais	nous savons	
tu sais	vous savez	
il sait	ils savent	
elle sait	elles savent	
on sait		

sécher: to dry (è/é)		j'ai séché (avoir + séché)
je sèche	nous séchons	
tu sèches	vous séchez	
il sèche	ils sèchent	
elle sèche	elles sèchent	
on sèche		

présent | **passé composé**

sourire: to smile	
je souris	nous sourions
tu souris	vous souriez
il sourit	ils sourient
elle sourit	elles sourient
on sourit	

j'ai souri
(avoir + souri)

suivre: to follow	
je suis	nous suivons
tu suis	vous suivez
il suit	ils suivent
elle suit	elles suivent
on suit	

j'ai suivi
(avoir + suivi)

tenir: to hold	
je tiens	nous tenons
tu tiens	vous tenez
il tient	ils tiennent
elle tient	elles tiennent
on tient	

j'ai tenu
(avoir + tenu)

venir*: to come	
je viens	nous venons
tu viens	vous venez
il vient	ils viennent
elle vient	elles viennent
on vient	

je suis venu
(être + venu)

vivre: to live	
je vis	nous vivons
tu vis	vous vivez
il vit	ils vivent
elle vit	elles vivent
on vit	

j'ai vécu
(avoir + vécu)

présent		passé composé

voir: to see	
je vois	nous voyons
tu vois	vous voyez
il voit	ils voient
elle voit	elles voient
on voit	

j'ai vu
(avoir + vu)

vouloir: to want	
je veux	nous voulons
tu veux	vous voulez
il veut	ils veulent
elle veut	elles veulent
on veut	

j'ai voulu
(avoir + voulu)